CAMBRIDGE ORATIONS 1982 1993

James Diggle

CAMBRIDGE ORATIONS 1982–1993

A SELECTION

James Diggle

Reader in Greek and Latin, University of Cambridge
and Fellow of Queens' College

CAMBRIDGE
UNIVERSITY PRESS

CAMBRIDGE UNIVERSITY PRESS
Cambridge, New York, Melbourne, Madrid, Cape Town, Singapore, São Paulo, Delhi

Cambridge University Press
The Edinburgh Building, Cambridge CB2 8RU, UK

Published in the United States of America by Cambridge University Press, New York

www.cambridge.org
Information on this title: www.cambridge.org/9780521466189

© Cambridge University Press 1994

First published 1994
Re-issued in this digitally printed version 2009

A catalogue record for this publication is available from the British Library

ISBN 978-0-521-46618-9 paperback

SATIVOLAE
VXORI CARISSIMAE

CONTENTS

Contents

INTRODUCTION

In 1910 Sir John Edwin Sandys published the 531 speeches and fifty-eight letters which he had composed during his first thirty-three years as Orator (*Orationes et Epistolae Cantabrigienses (1876–1909)*). None of his successors have followed his example; but recent Orators at Oxford and Trinity College, Dublin, have published selections of their speeches: T. F. Higham, *Orationes Oxonienses Selectae* (1960), J. G. Griffith, *Oratiunculae Oxonienses Selectae* (1985), and J. V. Luce, *Orationes Dublinienses Selectae (1971–1990)* (1991). This volume contains fifty of the 102 speeches which I composed and delivered in the Senate House during the eleven years (1982–1993) when I was Orator.

I have often been asked about the origins, history and name of the Orator. Since no account exists, here is a brief essay.[1]

'The Orator's place (that you may understand what it is) is the finest place in the University ... for the Orator writes all the University Letters, makes all the Orations, be it to King, Prince, or whatever comes to the University.'[2] So it was in the beginning, and so it was when George Herbert was Orator (1619–1627).

Today the Orator has two duties, defined by Statute: 'He shall write addresses for presentation to the Sovereign and formal letters for presentation to other universities and institutions. He shall present to the Chancellor and University persons on whom the titles of degrees are conferred *honoris causa*.' In these past eleven years Cambridge has despatched formal letters to the Universities of Auckland, Bologna, Graz, Harvard, Heidelberg, Siena, Zaragoza, the Complutensian University of Madrid, and the Universities of Nihon and Waseda in Tokyo, to congratulate them on the celebration of an anniversary. If we wish to understand how the office of Orator first came into being, it is with the writing of letters that we must begin.

The office was founded by Statute in (probably) the year 1521.[3] The original Statute (which is undated) was written in what is known as The Junior Proctor's Book.[4] It is a lengthy Statute, and it tells an interesting tale, though it leaves some things unsaid which it obliges us to supply by conjecture. I shall quote the larger part and supply such commentary as it demands.[5] It begins in this way:

Since our public interest[6] has often been brought into danger owing to the want of letters imploring the aid of great men against our adversaries, who ought to have been opposed with such letters as our best protection, and each person has declined the trouble, partly on account of the small amount of reward, and partly through fear of the power and influence of those against whom the letters ought to have been written, we have at length resolved, as dutiful sons, to give aid to our mother University in this her difficulty; and so that our adversaries may not be able to come into personal collision with those who, as in duty they are bound, defend the cause of the University to the best of their power, we enact, ordain, and will, that *one public orator* shall be chosen, on whose shoulders shall devolve the burdens to be described in the following paragraphs, none of which he shall decline, but shall diligently sustain; to which intent we enact and will that he be bound by oath immediately on his admission.

'One public orator': three simple words, but not as simple as they seem. First, 'orator'. To us the word signifies 'speaker'; but not to the framers of the Statute, or not primarily. The noun is derived from the verb *orare*, 'beg, beseech, implore'. The Statute (as much of it as I have so far quoted) is concerned with the begging of aid, and it is concerned with the written, more than with the spoken, word. It had long been the custom of the University's officers, in petitions to the monarch or others whose favours they sought, to subscribe themselves as 'orators'.[7]

Second, the numeral 'one'. Again, it had long been the University's custom to employ in the composition of letters and petitions such of its members as possessed the necessary talent. The Proctors' accounts record many a payment for this piecemeal work. A single example: between the years 1483 and 1504 a frequent composer, who received a fee for each letter composed, was 'Caius Auberinus'. He also taught Latin, and was formerly believed to be an Italian humanist, but he has recently been identified as the English poet John Kay.[8]

Finally, the epithet 'public'. This signifies that the Orator acts on behalf of the whole University, not on behalf of himself or of any one College. It is not unique to the Orator. There was a time when Professors and lecturers and examinations were 'public'. Even the University Library was once the Public Library.[9] Today Oxford has a Public Orator. This was probably his title from his first appointment in 1564.[10] At all events, the Oxford Statutes of 1636 entitle him *Publicus Universitatis Orator*. But at Cambridge you will look in vain for a Public Orator in the Statutes as variously revised through the centuries. The title was, indeed, used in Cambridge, but perhaps not before the seventeenth century. Ralph Widdrington, resigning in 1673, calls himself Public

Orator.[11] And the title was already known to Thomas Fuller in 1655.[12] The *Cambridge University Calendar*, published annually from 1796, has Public Orator from the first, consistently throughout the nineteenth century, and for the last time in 1925–6. The *Reporter*, the University's official newspaper, last used the title on 12 July 1926, and suddenly, without warning, adopted the title Orator in the next issue on 11 August. This was the year in which the Statutes, after several years of deliberation, were radically revised.[13] I assume that the University authorities, in the course of these deliberations, had taken note of the discrepancy and thought it proper to bring other official publications into line with the Statutes. In 1932 the *Historical Register of the University of Cambridge, Supplement, 1921–30* declares: '"Public Orator" is out of use.' It is still, from time to time, heard in conversation or seen in print.

To return to the Statute: the University resolved to charge a single individual with tasks which formerly had been executed, in some degree, by a multitude of others, if others could be found, as sometimes they could not. And this it resolved at a time when its interests were threatened by unspecified adversaries, and when it needed all the favour it could get from the Crown and from others of influence. We are in (or near) the twelfth year of the reign of Henry VIII.[14]

The Statute proceeds to list the Orator's duties. First, he shall 'faithfully compose letters in the name of the University[15] against any persons whatsoever, even though they be his own friends, and in defence of any persons, though his own enemies'. Second, he shall assist the Vice-Chancellor and Proctors in soliciting the assistance of the King or the nobles. Third, he shall 'welcome all princes and nobles with a learned and elaborate speech'. Fourth, he shall 'go to any princes or nobles and faithfully plead before them the cause of the University against any adversaries, provided that the University furnish him with the expenses for himself and a servant and two horses'. Fifth and last, 'if he should learn of any plan formed against the University, by friend or foe, he shall at his earliest convenience give notice of it to the Vice-Chancellor and Proctors, and assist them with any advice by which he thinks that the University may avoid any dangers that may be impending therefrom'.

So much for the Duties. Now the Privileges. They remained unaltered for much longer than the duties, and even today a vestige of them remains. Since the Orator is to be 'the assertor and defender of public liberty', the Statute grandly declares, 'it is right that such a man should be held in honour'. And so the Orator, if a Master of Arts, shall be ranked above all other Masters, immediately after the Doctors of Law and Medicine; he shall walk alone in processions and sit in a separate place at meetings.[16] In addition to these marks of honour he shall be dispensed from certain obligations: 'attendance at masses, obsequies,[17] and even statutable congregations'. In granting this dispensation the Statute acknowledges that the Orator 'seems likely to be exposed, on behalf of the University, to the resentment of many', and to be 'occasionally too much involved in his own business' to be always at the University's call. Finally, he shall be paid forty shillings a year – not so much as a salary, but rather to cover the costs of hiring a deputy when he cannot discharge his duties in person. The office was ever, as Thomas Fuller remarked, 'a place of more honour than profit'.[18]

The Statute also declares that subsequent Orators, after the first, shall be appointed for a period of seven years,[19] with the provision that they must remain resident in the University. At the time when the Statute was framed the first Orator had already been appointed, for the Statute informs us, almost casually, that he is 'Master Croke', and that Croke shall hold the office as long as he likes provided that he remains resident. What is more, if Croke should cease to be resident, he shall 'enjoy all his privileges, everywhere and always', and, if he should return, he shall 'rank immediately above the Orator, except that the Orator of the time shall preserve his office and enjoy his privileges, just as if Croke was not here'.

Who then was Richard Croke, first Orator, and why was he treated with such favour? Scholar of King's, lecturer in Greek at Leipzig, esteemed by Erasmus, recalled to Cambridge to be lecturer in Greek then Orator, Fellow of St John's,[20] despatched to Italy as agent of the King, where he went by the name of John of Flanders and sought by bribery to buy compliance with the royal divorce, Canon of King Henry VIII College (later Christ Church) in Oxford, witness for the prosecution at the trial of Cranmer, he died, Rector of Long Buckby, Northamptonshire, in 1558. He deserves the University's favour, claims the Statute, for two reasons: 'because he first introduced Greek literature among us, and because he is beloved by the King, in whose name he was strongly commended to us by the principal nobles'. The second reason has more truth than the first, for the first suggests that Cambridge had already forgotten Erasmus less than a decade after his departure for Basle.[21]

The Statute finally enacts that Croke's successors shall be chosen at a full congregation of senior members by the majority vote of those present, who shall not be 'constrained by the common resolution of the colleges'.[22] The Orator is to be 'a man of natural eloquence, equally skilled in Greek and Latin'.

The procedure for electing the Orator was changed by the Statutes of Elizabeth I in 1570.[23] These Statutes prescribed that all University 'officers' (of whom the Orator is one) should be elected according to the procedure laid down for the election of the Vice-Chancellor. The Heads of House are to nominate two candidates, and the Senate [Masters or higher graduates, whether resident or not] is to elect one of them.[24] In this lies the origin of the present procedure: 'The Regent House [residents only] shall elect as Orator one of two members of the Senate nominated by the Council.'

These and other rights granted by the Elizabethan Statutes to the Heads of House were much resented in the centuries which followed.[25] In 1673 some members of the Senate claimed the right to elect as Orator whomsoever they wished. They appealed to the Chancellor, the Duke of Buckingham. The Chancellor suggested that the Senate should accept the nominations of the Heads on this occasion but should be at liberty to pursue their claim for an open election in future. He then recommended to the Heads that they should nominate Isaac Craven of Trinity and Henry Paman of St John's, whom he believed to be the candidates favoured by the Senate. But the Heads nominated Paman and Ralph Sanderson, another Johnian. Members of the Senate protested, Isaac Newton among them, and proceeded to cast 121 votes for Craven and only ninety-eight for Paman, whom, none the less, the Vice-Chancellor declared elected.[26]

Elections were frequently robust affairs: voters were canvassed, pamphlets issued, battle-lines drawn, even to the end of the last century. Richard Jebb, elected in 1869, writes to his mother: 'The whole of the powerful Trinity influence was set in work for me; men came up from all parts of the country, not caring a straw whether Jones or Smith was Public Orator, but determined to vote for the College ticket; and from London we got down a special train with about 200 Cambridge barristers and clergymen.'[27] When Sandys was elected in 1876, 'Some hundreds of non-resident Members of the Senate came to Cambridge to record their votes, and the town presented quite an animated appearance. Both the Great Eastern and the Great Northern Railway Companies ran a late train to London, stopping at intermediate stations. At most of the colleges entertainment was provided for the out-voters.'[28] In the 1869 election 910 votes were cast (Jebb 528, A. Holmes 382),[29] in the 1876 election 1288 (Sandys 701, C. W. Moule 587).[30] On Sandys' retirement in 1920 A. E. Housman was invited by his friends to stand as Orator. He replied in characteristic style: 'Not if the stipend were £150,000 instead of £150 would I be Public Orator. I could not discharge the duties of the office without abandoning all other duties and bidding farewell to such peace of mind as I possess.'[31] In that year the votes cast were 306 (T. R. Glover 162, W. T. Vesey 144).[32] These days, when the electorate is restricted to the Regent House,[33] the affair is more muted. In 1939 the votes cast were 130 (W. K. C. Guthrie 67, L. P. Wilkinson 63).

Something of the earlier robustness in electioneering rubbed off on the ceremonies themselves. Registrary Romilly records the events of 1835. 'Then followed the Duke of Wellington who was received with a round of applause & reiterated shouts which seemed absolutely interminable: the effect was certainly very fine; & it so much worked upon one's feelings that it produced a choking sensation in one's throat. The Orator's speech about the D. of W. was much admired, especially the part about mingling the Civic Ivy with the Military Laurels.'[34] In 1870 Jebb presented a Greek Archbishop. 'Long before the hour fixed for the commencement of the proceedings, the privileged began to flock in, and at last all the efforts of the officials to stem the pressure from without were of no avail, and a multitude forced their way in pell-mell. The galleries had long been crowded with undergraduates, who wiled away the time with their usual vagaries'; and the Orator's speech was punctuated by 'commentary and criticism from the undergraduates', while 'the countenance of the Archbishop and his confrères evinced some amusement at English undergraduate life, but none of them for a moment departed from an almost statuesque dignity'.[35]

The honorary degree has a long history, and, like the office of Orator, its nature has changed in time. When the University resolved in 1492–3 that John Skelton, 'a poet crowned with laurel in lands beyond the sea [at Louvain in 1492] and at Oxford [in 1488], shall receive the same decoration from ourselves',[36] what he received was presumably the equivalent of an honorary degree. In the following centuries honorary degrees were awarded in profusion to civil and ecclesiastical dignitaries and nominees of the Crown. In 1717, during a visit by George I, the degree of Doctor of Law was conferred on twenty-seven members of the royal retinue.[37] The Orator might count himself fortunate that it was not his duty, on such occasions, to praise each honorand. Until recent times there was available a multitude of honorary degrees, whether 'complete' or 'titular'.[38] Nowadays most honorary degrees are titular ('Titles of degrees may be granted *honoris causa* to members of the Royal Family, to British subjects who are of conspicuous merit or have done good service to the State or to the University, and to foreigners of distinction'), and the recipient of a titular degree (in contrast to the recipient of a complete degree) does not become a member of the Senate. Normally eight such degrees (of Doctor of Divinity, or Law, of Science, or Letters, or Music) are awarded each year at a ceremony in June. As an especial mark of honour a further ceremony may be arranged, as it was when honorary degrees were conferred on the King and Queen of Spain in 1988 and on the President of India in 1993. In addition, the title of the degree of Master of Arts is sometimes conferred on local persons, for long service to the University or City of Cambridge.

W. K. C. Guthrie (Orator 1939–1957) captured the essence of the Orator's art in a striking image: 'To produce a good speech of the length customary nowadays calls for a kind of gem-cutting in words, a complete picture, preferably not lacking in detail, within the bezel of a ring. This in itself, incidentally, is an all-sufficient reason for retaining Latin as the medium, since it provides a material of unexampled hardness and brilliance in which to execute this lapidary work.'[39] Since Guthrie's time the art has gained a new dimension, for the Orator must provide an English translation for the audience to read while he is orating. No longer shall we hear the like of the exchange that was heard between two honorands in 1920, Lloyd George and Sir Donald Maclean: Ll. G. 'Did you understand what the Public Orator said about you?' – D. M. 'Not very well. I don't know the new pronunciation. Did *you* understand what he said about you? – Ll. G. 'I don't know, but the gist was that considering I'm a Welshman I'm a fairly honest man – but they always exaggerate.'[40]

An English version can be, and should be, more than a crib. A good Latin style is very different from a good English style, and declamatory Latin (if it is to have the rhythms and the rhetorical mannerisms of Cicero) is quite unlike readable English. Furthermore, it is desirable to diverge in the English from the Latin, where a point can be made appropriately in one language but not in the other, or where a similar effect (such as humour) can be gained simultaneously in both languages, but by different means.

Unlike Sandys, but like Higham, Griffith and Luce, I publish a selection, not a complete collection of my speeches. To those honorands who could not be included, if they are disappointed, I offer my apologies.

As Higham said, in explaining his own selection, 'Exclusions are due to no such invidious criterion as the relative interest and importance of the honorands, but simply to the need for variety of theme and treatment.'

I acknowledge with gratitude many debts: to Professor Christopher Brooke for historical advice; to Dr Elisabeth Leedham-Green for assistance in the Archives; to Mr A. G. Lee, Dr J. C. McKeown and Dr S. P. Oakley, who contributed occasional emendations at the time when the speeches were written. Too many to name are the friends, colleagues and correspondents who gave me their advice and instruction on persons whom I did not know or matters which I did not understand. This book is dedicated, in acknowledgement of a very special debt, to my wife Sedwell. She listened to successive drafts of the English versions, before they were first printed, and, with her acute ear, saved me from many a wrong note, and often gave me a truer one: *nobis ingenium, nobis dedit ore rotundo | Musa loqui.*

NOTES

BIBLIOGRAPHY AND ABBREVIATIONS OF MAIN WORKS CITED

Cooper	C. H. Cooper, *Annals of Cambridge* (Cambridge 1842–1908)
Documents	*Documents relating to the University and Colleges of Cambridge* (Royal Commission, London 1852), vol. 1
Emden	A. B. Emden, *A Biographical Register of the University of Cambridge to 1500* (Cambridge 1963)
Grace Book A	S. M. Leathes (ed.), *Grace Book* A (Cambridge 1897)
Grace Book B	M. Bateson (ed.), *Grace Book* B (Cambridge 1903–5)
Grace Book Γ	W. G. Searle (ed.), *Grace Book* Γ (Cambridge 1908)
Hackett	M. B. Hackett, *The Original Statutes of Cambridge University: The Text and its History* (Cambridge 1970)
Heywood (1840)	J. Heywood, *Collection of Statutes for the University and Colleges of Cambridge* (London 1840)
Heywood (1855)	J. Heywood, *Early Cambridge University and College Statutes, in the English Language* (London 1855)
Lamb	J. Lamb, *A Collection of Letters, Statutes, and other Documents, from the Manuscript Library of Corpus Christi College* (London 1838)
Leader	D. R. Leader, *A History of the University of Cambridge: vol. 1, The University to 1546* (Cambridge 1988)
Mullinger	J. B. Mullinger, *The University of Cambridge from the earliest Times to ... 1535* (Cambridge 1873–1911)

1 *The Historical Register of the University of Cambridge ... to the Year 1910* (ed. J. R. Tanner, Cambridge 1917) 47–50 gives a complete list of Orators, down to Sandys, with a few biographical notes.

2 *The Works of George Herbert*, ed. F. E. Hutchinson (Oxford 1941) 369. Lest Herbert's editor mislead others, when he says that, on his election, Herbert 'put on the Orator's habit, received the Orator's book and lamp, and took his place next to the Doctors' (p. xxix), I had better say that Orators do not inherit lamps. When Herbert writes to his successor R. Creighton 'iube Thorndick nostrum ... librum tibi Oratorium lampademque tradat' (p. 470), he is adopting an image from Lucretius 2.79.

3 The date traditionally assigned to the office is 1522. This is based on an entry in the Proctors' accounts for the academic year 1522–3, which record a payment of forty shillings 'pro stipendio Magistri Crooke [sic] oratoris' (*Grace Book* B II.106). This is the

first time that Croke is anywhere referred to as Orator. Leader 298 suggests that the office was established in 1519, citing in support the entry for 1519–20 (p. 84), a payment of twenty shillings to Croke for a purpose unspecified. The next payment was made in 1520–1, also twenty shillings, 'pro eius stipendio in vesperiis' (p. 92). It is tempting to interpret this payment, at least, in the light of the Statute (*Documents* 433, Heywood (1855) 145), which prescribes payment of the Orator's stipend in two instalments, 'quadraginta solidi ... viginti scilicet in die vesperiarum et viginti ad festum natalis Domini', twenty shillings at 'vespers' and twenty at Christmas ('vespers', in late June or early July, is the first day of 'inception', the exercise leading to admission as M.A.: G. Peacock, *Observations on the Statutes of the University of Cambridge* (London 1841) Appendixes A and B, Hackett 126–7, 206–7, Leader 102–5). The two payments of 1519–20 and 1520–1 would make up an annual stipend, provided that they were made in consecutive half years. This requires that the vespers payment of 1520–1 was made in the summer of 1520, not of 1521. But in that case there will be a gap of one year before the next payment, in 1521–2, forty shillings 'pro suo annuo stipendio' (p. 101). I do not believe that Croke was Orator as early as 1519–20, because piecemeal payments for the composition of letters are still being made both to him in Michaelmas 1519 (p. 75) and to others in Lent and Easter 1520 (pp. 76, 83). The payment in 1521–2 does probably refer to the Orator's stipend, since the same formula (omitting specific reference to the Orator) is used in 1523–4 (p. 115). And I suspect that the twenty shillings paid at vespers in 1520–1 (the first payment specifically called a 'stipend') was the very first payment made to the Orator and was made in the summer of 1521. What, then, of the twenty shillings paid in 1519–20? This must be examined in the light of the next earlier payment made to Croke, £4 in 1518–19, again for an unspecified purpose (p. 69). We might be tempted to suggest that this is a payment to Croke as lecturer, since the termly payment for lecturing was £1.6s.8d. (made both to the Latin lecturer (see above, p. x) and to the lecturer in mathematics: *Grace Book* A 219–20, B I. 196, II. 45–6, and elsewhere), that is £4 per annum (B II. 59, 66, 70, 106, and elsewhere). But there is no record that the University ever paid Croke for lecturing. His lecturer's stipend was paid by Henry VIII, at least in 1520, when the accounts of the Royal Household record a payment of £5 to 'Mr Croke, reading Greek at Cambridge' (*Letters and Papers, foreign and domestic, of the Reign of Henry VIII*, 3.1 (ed. J. S. Brewer, London 1867) 409). In fact the payments of £4 and twenty shillings appear to have been loans. For in 1519–20 (p. 80) and 1520–1 (p. 91) we find that Croke owes the University £3.6s.8d. In Easter 1520 he repays £1.13s.4d. (p. 81). The residual debt of £3.6s.8d. after the repayment of £1.13s.4d. indicates that the original debt was £5, and it is reasonable to infer that this represents the £4 of 1518–19 and the twenty shillings of 1519–20.

4 On which see Hackett 290–3.

5 The Latin text is given in *Documents* 431–4 (p. 432, under heading 4, for 'substituat' substitute 'substituet'). I have adopted, with some changes, the translation of Heywood (1855) 142–6, which supersedes Heywood (1840) 334–8.

6 'respublica' (for which Heywood's 'commonwealth' sounds the wrong note) I have translated 'public interest' in order to preserve the verbal link with 'public orator' and 'public liberty' which come shortly. In effect, 'public interest' means 'University interest', as will emerge from the following discussion.

7 To Richard, Duke of Gloucester (1483), 'Your true and daly Oratours the Universite of Cambrigge' (*Grace Book* A 172, Cooper I. 226), and, when he had assumed the crown, 'regem regum exorabimus fidelissimi oratores' (p. 171, Cooper I. 230); to Henry VII (1489), 'youre continuall Oratours the Provost and Scolars of youre College Roiall'

(Cooper I. 236); and (1491), 'we your dayly orators and faythfull subjects' (Cooper I. 240); to various judges (1506), 'Yo^r true orators the Universite of Camebrig' (Cooper I. 276). See also *Oxford English Dictionary*, 'Orator, 2'.

8 The identification has been made by Damian Leader. I am greatly indebted to Dr Leader for his generosity in allowing me to read the typescript of an article, due for later publication, in which he sets forth the evidence, and in allowing me to report his identification in advance of his own article. For earlier discussion of Caius Auberinus see R. Weiss, *Humanism in England during the Fifteenth Century* (3rd edn, Oxford 1967) 163, Emden 23, Leader 250.

9 See *Oxford English Dictionary*, 'Public, 3b'.

10 'The Office therefore of public Orator is not ... ancient in the University ..., it being then [before the time of Elizabeth I] the custom for the Chancellor or his Deputy to court or invite that person that was generally known to have an eloquent pen and tongue to write Epistles to great persons, and harangue it before them at their coming to the University ... But upon a strong rumour that the learned Queen Elizabeth would visit the University, an. 1564, ... a worthy person was then elected to keep the said place for term of life', Anthony Wood, *The History and Antiquities of the University of Oxford* 2 (ed. J. Gutch, Oxford 1796) 904. Wood's book was first published in a Latin translation (not his own) in 1674.

11 Archives, CUR 45.9.

12 *The History of the University of Cambridge from the Conquest to the Year 1634* (eds. M. Prickett and T. Wright, Cambridge 1840) 199.

13 C. N. L. Brooke, *A History of the University of Cambridge: vol. iv, 1870–1990* (Cambridge 1993) ch. 11.

14 On the relations between the Universities and the State during this period see J. K. McConica, *English Humanists and Reformation Politics under Henry VIII and Edward VI* (Oxford 1965).

15 In 1529–30 it was enacted that copies of the letters should henceforth be inscribed in an official register (*Grace Book* Γ 243, *Documents* 436, Heywood (1855) 148–9), which is now in the Archives (Lett. 1–3). Royalty was not always amused to be addressed in Latin. Catherine Parr in 1546: 'Your letters I have receyved presentyd on all your behalfes by Mr Doctour Smythe [(Sir) Thomas Smith, Orator 1537–42 (not 1538–4?, as sometimes stated: see *Grace Book* B II. 212, 216)] your discrete and lerned advocate. And as they be lately [Latinly] wrytyn wyche is so singnyfyed unto me by those that be lernyd in the laten tonge so (I knowe) you colde have utteryd your desyres and opinions famylyerlye in your vulgare tonge aptyste for my intelligence' (Lamb 71, Heywood (1840) 211, Leader 344).

16 Today the Orator is ranked in seniority next after the higher Doctors, next before them if he is a higher Doctor himself. In honorary degree processions he walks alongside the Vice-Chancellor and Registrary.

17 For these see Hackett 175, 216–17.

18 See n. 12. The payment was increased to £4 in 1528–9 (*Grace Book* Γ 237, *Documents* 436, Heywood (1840) 338, (1855) 148, Mullinger II. 37, Leader 298), in 1587 by the addition of fees payable by graduands (Cooper II. 446), and these additional payments were increased in 1613, when it was observed that the Orator's stipend was less than half that of his counterpart in Oxford (Cooper III. 60).

19 The restriction was soon rescinded or forgotten. George Day held office from 1528 to 1537. But Day's successors showed no disposition to prolong their tenures: fourteen were appointed in the next thirty-six years. The record for length is held by Sandys (forty-three

years), for brevity by C. Wordsworth (4 February to 27 April 1836), who resigned on being appointed headmaster of Harrow.

20 A later Fellow, Thomas Baker, writing in 1707, described him as 'an ambitious, envious and discontented wretch', and compared him unfavourably with his successor Day (who was to be Master of St John's), 'a much greater man than he, though the other made the louder noise' (*History of the College of St John the Evangelist* (ed. J. E. B. Mayor, Cambridge 1869) I. 97, 113).

21 For Croke's career see C. H. Cooper, *Athenae Cantabrigienses* 1 (Cambridge 1858) 177–80, Mullinger I. 527–41, 614–15, *Dictionary of National Biography* 5 (London 1908) 119–21, J. E. Sandys, *A History of Classical Scholarship* 2 (Cambridge 1908) 231, J. T. Sheppard, *Richard Croke: A Sixteenth Century Don* (Cambridge 1919), D. F. S. Thomson and H. C. Porter, *Erasmus and Cambridge* (Toronto 1963) 86–9, A. B. Emden, *A Biographical Register of the University of Oxford A.D. 1501 to 1540* (Oxford 1974) 151–2, P. G. Bietenholz and T. B. Deutscher (eds.), *Contemporaries of Erasmus: A Biographical Register of the Renaissance and Reformation* 1 (Toronto 1985) 359–60.

22 'It was a custom...for the votes of each individual member of a College to be given in the Senate according to the previous determination of the matter at issue by the majority of voices in his own College' (editorial note in *Documents* 434).

23 For the relation of these Statutes to their immediate predecessors see Hackett 303–5.

24 *Documents* 470–1, 478, Lamb 331–2, 327.

25 See D. A. Winstanley, *Unreformed Cambridge* (Cambridge 1935) ch. 1, *Early Victorian Cambridge* (Cambridge 1955) ch. 4.

26 Archives, CUR 45. 10–15; Cooper V. 469–70. For another such controversy in 1727 see J. H. Monk, *The Life of Richard Bentley, D.D.* (2nd edn, London 1830) 524–6, Cooper IV. 187, Winstanley, *Unreformed Cambridge* 341 n. 57.

27 Caroline Jebb, *Life and Letters of Sir Richard Claverhouse Jebb* (Cambridge 1907) 98.

28 A contemporary newspaper report (Archives, CUR 45.1, 54). See also N. G. L. Hammond, *Sir John Edwin Sandys 1844–1922* (Cambridge 1933) 38–9. For a bibliography on Sandys see P. G. Naiditch, *A. E. Housman at University College, London: The Election of 1892* (Leiden 1988) 209 n. 1.

29 For these figures (which correct the officially published figures) see CUR 45. 40a.

30 CUR 45. 1, 53.

31 *The Letters of A. E. Housman*, ed. H. Mass (London 1971) 170.

32 Housman supported Vesey (CUR 45. 2, 5), for whose adulation of Housman see Naiditch (n. 28 above) 168 n. 4.

33 The restriction to resident members was proposed and rejected in 1878 (Winstanley, *Later Victorian Cambridge* (Cambridge 1947) 289–91, 296), approved in 1926 (Brooke (n. 13 above) 351).

34 J. P. T. Bury, *Romilly's Cambridge Diary 1832–42* (Cambridge 1967) 81.

35 *Cambridge Chronicle*, 19 February 1870. See also Caroline Jebb (n. 27 above) 100.

36 *Grace Book* B I.54 'Conceditur Johanni Skelton poete in partibus transmarinis atque Oxonie laurea ornato ut aput nos eadem decoretur' (mistranslated by Leader 105). See also Emden 529–30, Leader 119.

37 Monk (n. 26 above) 359–60, Cooper IV. 148–9.

38 For the changing nature of honorary degrees and of those entitled to them see A. Wall, *The Ceremonies observed in the Senate House of the University of Cambridge* (ed. H. Gunning, Cambridge 1828) 211–16, Cooper III. 582, IV. 418, Sandys, *Orationes...* vi–vii, Winstanley, *Unreformed Cambridge* 79–83, *Early Victorian Cambridge* 152–3, 167, 246–7, 338, Leader 40.

39 I quote from a private journal, by permission of the late Mrs A. M. Guthrie. See also my remarks in *Classical Review* 37 (1987) 92.

40 H. G. Wood, *Terrot Reaveley Glover* (Cambridge 1953) 130–1. There is an excellent assessment of Glover's orations by R. J. Getty, *The Eagle* (St John's College Magazine) 51 (1939) 211–36.

THE ORATIONS

'QVIS IGNORAT, ei qui mathematici uocantur, quanta in obscuritate rerum et quam recondita in arte et multiplici subtilique uersentur?' ita M. Tullius.[1] uiri itaque merita quem artis geometricae omnes antistitem agnoscunt – geometricae dico? immo ingenium nullis mathematices limitibus consaeptum ad quaestiones etiam physicorum spinosissimas soluendas attendit – si ego, orator numerorum prorsus ignarus, explicare coner, edepol, sicut Socrates olim, in βυθὸν φλυαρίας incidam.[2] cuius operis si capax essem, titulum praefigere paginae liminari debeam: ΑΓΕΩΜΕΤΡΗΤΟΣ ΜΗΔΕΙΣ ΕΙΣΙΤΩ. quid ergo? numeris aliunde quaesitis paullo maiora canamus.

> Euclides πρῶτος εὑρετής geometriae cluebat,
> qui inuenit rhombos et quadras, symmetriae consortes,
> figuras aequicrurias, quid prosient diuinae
> trianguli concordiae, uir uere τετράγωνος.
> Euclides alter nunc adest, qui spatia perscrutatur
> nec formam nec symmetriam nec finem habentia ullum.
> uibrationem si potes chordai demetiri
> uel nutum, cum quassaueris, pultis coagulatae,
> si terna derna triciens quot sint scis computare
> ubi mutarunt locum pedes cum gymnico cerebro,
> si in ludo calculi cales nec obuius uenire
> pauescis 'solitario' uel formulae Riemanni,
> ad summam si nomen tibist Thales aut Archimedes,
> intellegas quid indicet fortasse Lex Atiyae.

Hoc unum, mihi sane explicatu facilius uobis intellectu promptius, non silendum: mathematicos quotquot ubique sint huius in uerba magistri iurare, quos non tantum operum suorum praestantia deuinxerit sed etiam instinctu quodam diuino excitatos ad sui aemulationem instigauerit.

Praesento uobis in Collegiis Sanctae et Indiuiduae Trinitatis et Pembrochiano olim Socium, quem Collegium utrumque Socium honoris causa adsciuit, olim apud nos mathematices praelectorem, nunc apud Oxonienses in Instituto Mathematico professorem, aureo nomismate a Societate Regia, nomismate Fieldsiano ab Vniuerso Mathematicorum Conuentu ornatum, Equitem Auratum,

MICHAELEM FRANCISCVM ATIYAH

[1] Cicero, *De Oratore*, 1. 3. 10.
[2] Plato, *Parmenides*, 130 d.

'EVERYONE *knows*', *said Cicero,* '*that people who are called mathe-maticians deal in matters of incomprehensible complexity and subtlety.*' *If I, an innumerate orator, were to attempt to expound the achievements of a man who is acknowledged to be the leading geometrician of his day* (*did I say geometrician? such a label does him less than justice, for he ranges as far as the thorniest problems in mathematical physics*), *I fear that I might fall* (*in the words of Socrates*) *into an* '*abyss of twaddle*'. *If I were even capable of a serious exposition, I should have to prefix to it the notice which stood at the entrance of Plato's Academy:* RESTRICTED ACCESS – GEOMETERS ONLY. *Let me try a type of* '*number*' *with which I am more familiar.*

> *The geometry we learned at school was labelled Euclidean:*
> *It dealt with squares and rhomboids and with shapes isoscelean,*
> *All regular, symmetrical; it showed us what the use is*
> *Of the transcendental harmony of squared hypotenuses.*
> *But then Sir Michael came along, to baffle comprehension,*
> *With spaces a-symmetrical explored in nth dimension.*
> *If you can map the motion of a cello-string vibrating*
> *Or the mesmerizing wobble of a jelly undulating,*
> *If you can do equations whether simple or quadratic*
> *While standing on your head, because your brain's so acrobatic,*
> *If you're a wiz at calculus and don't get in a panic*
> *When face to face with solitons or formulas Riemannic,*
> *In short, if you're a Newton or a Hardy, have no fe-ar:*
> *You'll understand* (*maybe*) *the Index Theorem of Atiyah.*

What may be more easily comprehended and more plainly expressed is the influence which he holds over a whole generation of mathematicians, not only by the quality of his own work but no less by his abounding enthusiasm and fecundity of ideas, which have been the inspiration of a school of disciples the world over.

I present to you a former Research Fellow of Trinity and Teaching Fellow of Pembroke, of both of which Colleges he is now an Honorary Fellow, a former University Lecturer in Mathematics, who is now Royal Society Research Professor at the Mathematical Institute in Oxford, a holder of the Gold Medal of the Royal Society and the Fields Medal of the International Congress of Mathematicians,

Sir MICHAEL FRANCIS ATIYAH, M.A., PH.D.

RARA INSEQVITVR AVIS, quae, licet insulae nostrae indigena sit, terras tamen longinquas frequentat. uiderunt enim siluae Guianenses, uiderunt culmina Himalayensia, uidit Amazonas siue Andibus prosiliens siue mari Atlantico sese immergens. natiuam quippe curiositatem insito omnium animalium amore conditam habet, adeo ut cum gorillis bacchari, cum dasypodidis iocari, aptenodytarum in familiaritate uersari gaudeat. si quando ad patriam redit, non ζωιοτροφεῖον, non campos late patentes, sed potius cistellulam ad unum latus uitream pro domicilio sibi deligit. illuc, cum tantam scientiae famam collegerit, tali sit ingenii comitate, tam mellita suauiloquentia, immensa spectatrix hominum multitudo conuenire solet, quo speciosa peregrinationum miracula auribus et oculis exhauriat. per menses tres continuos obstipuerunt omnes et intenti tenebant ora, dum animantium uitam exponit πάντων ὅσσα τε γαῖαν ἔπι πνείει τε καὶ ἕρπει,[1] et sic naturae legibus edictum esse demonstrat, ut debilissimum quodque genus deficere, superesse ualidissimum debeat. laudamus, adclamamus, ne fabularum sit intermissio postulamus. mox renouato sermone narrauit φυσίζοον αἶαν, qua opum largitate plantarum animaliumque copiam nutriat et educet. ostendit hydromedusam incredibili cum eurythmia natantem, ostendit ranunculum caerulipedem proci partes agentem, exporrecta fronte seriorum praeceptor, dulcibus utilia miscens, εὐφιλόπαις καὶ γεραροῖς ἐπίχαρτος.[2]

Hodie nido suo reducem laeti excipimus, puniceo pennarum tegmine indutam, cum auolabit, prosecuturi.

Praesento uobis Excellentissimi Ordinis Imperii Britannici Commendatorem, Magistrum in Artibus, Collegii de Clare olim alumnum nunc honoris causa Socium,

DAVIDEM FRIDERICVM ATTENBOROUGH

[1] Homer, *Iliad*, 17. 447.
[2] Aeschylus, *Agamemnon*, 721–2.

NEXT *comes a rare bird. Although a native of our island, he is a frequent visitor to far-off climes. He has been spotted in the forests of Guyana, on the summits of the Himalayas, and following the Amazon from the Andes to the Atlantic. Inspired with a natural curiosity and a love of his fellow creatures, he has played with armadillos, cavorted with gorillas, and the ice-bound penguins count him their friend. Returning at intervals to his homeland, he has found that the habitat which suits him best is not a zoo nor the wild, but a glass-fronted box; and such is the fame of his knowledge and the charm of his manner and the sweetness of his voice that millions have gathered before him to hear the wondrous tales and see the wondrous sights brought back from his travels. For three whole months he held us spellbound by his glorious account of Life on Earth. He showed how each species evolved, the fitter surviving, the weaker declining. We cried out for more. He told how the Living Planet nourishes the multitude of plants and animals. He showed us the beauty of a jellyfish in motion, showed us the courtship of the blue-footed frog, mingling instruction with pleasure, a model of learning worn lightly, for young and old a delight.*

Today we rejoice that he has returned to the nest which fledged him, and that when he takes wing again he will wear a new and scarlet plumage.

I present to you

DAVID FREDERICK ATTENBOROUGH, M.A., C.B.E.,

Honorary Fellow of Clare College.

ADSTAT VIR ΠΟΛΥѠΝΥΜΟΣ: audit enim poeta, bibliothecarius, professor, sed ante omnia fabellarum auctor, angustis quidem terminis circumscriptarum sed mirae inuentionis fecundissimarum. quis scit an antiquae superstitioni fidem habendam esse demonstrauerit? scilicet ad superos regressum modo Michaelem de Cervantes, modo Edgarum Allanum Poe, modo Valerium Francogallorum, modo Georgium Berkeley huius sub persona credas delitescentem. erunt fortasse qui huius libellos φωνάεντα συνετοῖσιν dicere et ἑρμανέων χατίζειν arbitrentur, propterea quod multifariae doctrinae copiosus usitatas de essentia, de tempore, de cognitione notiones exploret atque in ancipiti relinquat. erunt qui ab eis animo anxio et sibi diffidenti euadant, cum mundum depingere gaudeat modo uel horti instar in quo sunt semitae in aeternum bifurcae uel bibliothecae quae libros innumerabiles complectitur temerario litterarum ordine inscriptos, modo solitae temporum rationis adeo expertem ut saeculum minimo temporis puncto exactum, pusillum interuallum plurimos per annos protractum esse uideatur. alii filum quo errabunda e labyrintho uestigia expediant consulto hunc sibi impertiisse suspicantur, ubi hoc de philosophis Tloenensibus praedicauerit, non eos quae uera uel uerisimilia sed quae plena sint obstupefactionis indagare.

Quod praecipuam cum Anglis et scriptoribus Anglicis consuetudinem habet non mirum, cum matris e Staffordiae Comitatu oriundae ex filio nepos sit. paucis uero abhinc annis coram consessu Cantabrigiensium abundanti contionatus est, quos oratione perquam sapienti et animi candore deuinxit. postea, cum eidem uenerationis suae pignus testari studerent, oratorem auscultauit de oratore de se olim fabulato fabulantem, multis quidem audientium obscurum, sed ipsi sibi planum et pellucidum.

Praesento uobis uirum inter Excellentissimi Ordinis Imperii Britannici Equites Commendatores honoris causa adscriptum,

GEORGIVM LVDOVICVM BORGES

T HERE *stands before you a man who has been known by many names:*
poet, librarian, professor, but, above all, writer of fictions, miniature
in scale but miraculous in invention. Perhaps he has proved the truth of
ancient myths: for in his person now Cervantes, now Poe, now Valéry, now
the philosopher Berkeley seem to be born again. Some may find him
difficult, because, drawing on vast stores of curious learning in many
languages, he challenges their assumptions about being and time and
perception. Some may find him disturbing, because he writes of a world
conceived now as a garden of paths that fork endlessly, now as a library
of books indefinite in number, lettered at random, a world in which
centuries may seem minutes and seconds seem years. Others suspect that
he left them a clue to his purpose when he wrote, of the metaphysicians of
Tlön, that they seek not for truth, nor for likelihood, but for astonishment.

He has a special attachment to England and to its writers: a grand-
mother from Staffordshire is responsible in part. At Cambridge they once
invited him to talk to a large assembly, and he held it enthralled by his
simple humanity and profoundly wise talk about many things. Later they
invited him again, to tell him how much they valued him, and he listened to
an orator reciting a story, which perplexed some of its hearers, because the
orator ended by telling how he had once told a story about an orator who
had told a story about him once. But he was not perplexed.

I present to you

JORGE LUIS BORGES, HON. K.B.E.

INCLINANTIBVS in bellum nationibus Europaeis, dux nouus Italiae diuo Augusto Caesari decessori sollemnia honorum bis millesima indixit, sese uenditandi uirtutibus alienis, adstrepente apparitorum uulgo. erat ea tempestate Oxoniae iuuenis, Noua Zelandia recens profectus, qui illud spectaculum inrisui habuit. quippe Vergilii Horatiique laudes imperatorias inter inania esse perspexerat, rem publicam in imperium ruentem libro mox expositurus, detecto principe subdolo et per nomen pacis omnium rerum cupitore. quae uitae forensis tum condicio callebat: obtentu liberae ciuitatis non inter plebem patresque certatum honestis factionibus et citra immodestiam, sed cuncta proceribus, quanto quis regendi auarior, subiecta, ui ambitu rapina grassantibus, incertum necessitudine magis sanguinis et honorum commercio sociatis an propter conscientiam caedis. singulos potentium ac nobilium inquisiuit: hunc unde ortus, illum cui genti matrimonio iunctus. tu, rogitauit, in quas adscitus partes honorum cupidine? dum caelo deum detrahit, deabus adscripsit Prosopographiam.

Primum hoc facinus noui inter historicos principatus. inde commentarios sescentos conscripsit, quibus quinque uolumina post non suffecerunt, et libros de Tacito Sallustio Ouidio, excussa etiam de Caesaribus historia, intellecto quae Fratrum Arualium arcana. ut immensum studiorum curriculum perstringam, hoc in primis praestare instituit, non anfractus ciuilium institutionum enucleare, non de causis rerum subtiliter philosophari, nec de uita uictuque incognitae rusticorum molis reddere rationes, sed homines perinde factorum claritudine et scriptis insignes e litterarum lapidumque memoria ad uitam reuocatos repraesentare, nunc antiqui annalium auctoris praeciso atque minaci stilo, nunc uberiorem orationis copiam ab imperii uergentis scriptore nostrati mutuatus.

Praesento uobis historiae antiquae apud Oxonienses Professorem Camdensem emeritum, Equitem Auratum, Ordini insigniter Meritorum adscitum,

RONALDVM SYME

A S WAR APPROACHED, *a young man in Oxford, fresh from New Zealand, looked on in scorn and without illusion as the Leader of Italy decreed the celebration of a bimillennium for his deified ancestor Caesar Augustus and bathed in the effulgence of borrowed grandeur, to the pious plaudits of a black-shirted throng. The nascent historian was soon to strip from the idealized brows of the earliest Emperor the garland first hung there by Virgil and Horace. His book would tell of the Roman Revolution, when the Republic became an Empire, and a ruthless and fraudulent youth founded a tyranny in the name of peace. He had divined the true substance of political life in the dying Republic. Behind the sham and screen of a constitution subsisted no polite conflict of parties and programmes, nor the honest contention of Senate and People, but the thirst for power, wealth and glory of unscrupulous dynasts, linked by the commerce of services and favours and the sanguinary bonds of family and slaughter. He summoned the whole aristocracy to answer his questions. From what town do you come? To whom are you linked by ties of marriage? To which faction, in hope of advancement? He dethroned a god and enthroned a goddess: Prosopography.*

This was the first intimation of his ascendancy. Innumerable papers accrued, for whose subsequent collection five volumes have not sufficed; and studies of Tacitus, Sallust, Ovid, that deceitful brew the Historia Augusta, those quaint priestly figures the Arval Brethren. If a summary estimation be permitted of productions so wide and various, we may say that he accounts it to be his prime avocation, not to scrutinize curiously the niceties of constitutions, nor to speculate abstractly on the causes of events, nor to tabulate precisely the habits and numbers of voiceless earth-coloured rustics, but to illumine the men who made the history of Rome and the motives and manners of those who recorded their actions, and to re-create and revoke them into new life and voice from the silent testimony of letters and stones, in a style incarnating now the terse and sinister annalist of the Caesars, now the rotund and ampler periods of the modern chronicler of their decline and fall.

I present to you

Sir RONALD SYME, o.m.,

Emeritus Camden Professor of Ancient History in the University of Oxford.

QVOD PRIMARIAS cantrices Itali diuas nuncupare solent, hoc uos, doctores primarii, tamquam extraneam uaniloquentiam forsitan explodere uelitis. ego equidem diuam praesentem laudibus extollendi certus sum: ἑκὰς ergo ἑκὰς ὅστις ἄμουσος. haec enim illud supra mortale in se habet, quod naturam suam musices modis tam penitus scit immergere atque implicare ut audientes non uoce tantum sed omnibus etiam animi et corporis adfectionibus adpellare, ad nouam uoluptatis uim, nouam perceptionis prolectare uideatur. uidelicet, dum caua solatur aegrum testudine amorem, libenter hanc credimus

> tigris comitesque siluas
>
> ducere et riuos celeres morari.[1]

nec minus in hac personatam abundantiam admiramur, quae proteruam Dorabellam tam sollerter quam Alcestin flebiliter fidelem repraesentet, tam bene delicatam indolem Carlottae quam Iulii Caesaris robur ac neruos. et quid quod, dum fabula Callistonis agebatur, in scaenam prodiit modo Iuppiter, modo Diana? subit feminarum lamentantium nobilis pompa: subeunt Penelope, Octauia, Vitellia, Dido, Lucretia, subit denique quae uel maxime nos commouit Maria Scotorum Regina, exsul exspes splendida dolore.

Scripsit haec ipsa uocem suam sibi a Deo non mancipio esse commodatam uerum hac condicione, ut eius fructum perciperent quam plurimi. nimirum, dum sublimes Iohannis Sebastiani modos, dum Angeli uerba somnianti Gerontio interpretatur, pro certo habemus, si quid in caelo musices futurum sit, huius nos uocem audituros esse caelestem. quod autem non rursus hanc pulpita uidebunt lugemus ipsi, lugent pulpita, et Mimnermi illa τίς δὲ βίος sine te τί δὲ τερπνόν suspirare cui non uenit in mentem? mehercule, si mihi liquidum carmen chordasque loquentes Deus secundet, et ipse cantilenae illi statim incumbam, nemini obliuiscendae modo ab hac decantatam audiuerit,

> Ἔρχεο, Μοῖσα, πάλιν, πάλιν ἔρχεο, Μοῖσα ποθεινά.

Praesento uobis Excellentissimi Ordinis Imperii Britannici Dominam Commendatricem,

JANET ABBOTT BAKER

---

[1] Horace, *Odes*, 3. 11. 13–14. The English version adapts Dryden, *A Song for Saint Cecilia's Day, 1687,* 48–9.

THE ITALIANS give the name 'goddess' to their prima donnas. Some prim dons may dismiss this as foreign affectation. Yet, if there is any in this assembly that hath no music in himself, nor is not moved with concord of sweet sounds, let him depart, for it is of a goddess that I speak. She has that quality not given to mortal singers, to become the music itself, so that it speaks to us not from her voice alone but from her whole being, and draws forth a new, unexpected, intenser response. When, as Orpheus, she pours forth her heart for her lost beloved, we half believe that the beasts will be tame, the rivers still, and trees unrooted leave their place, sequacious of the lyre. We marvel at her infinite variety: skittish as Dorabella, a sadly faithful Alcestis; tenderly feminine as Charlotte, a heroic and manly Julius Caesar. And how miraculously she combined two extremes when in the same performance she played both Diana and Jupiter in 'La Calisto'. A pageant of noble and sorrowing women passes before us: Penelope, Octavia, Vitellia, Dido, Lucretia, last and perhaps most moving of all Mary Stuart, radiant in grief and despair.

'I believe', she has written, 'that my voice and power of communication through music were given to me by God, to be shared with others.' When we hear her interpret the sacred music of Bach, or the words of the Angel to the dreaming Gerontius, we know that, if there is music in heaven, it will be her celestial voice. We weep that the stage will see her no more. And which of her admirers has not sighed to himself, Che farò senza Euridice? Nay, had I Jubal's lyre or Miriam's tuneful voice, I too might cry, from that song of Berlioz (unforgettable to those who have heard her sing it), Reviens, reviens ma bien aimée.

I present to you

Dame JANET ABBOTT BAKER

KAI σημεῖον μέγα ὤφθη. plane pro miraculo habendum duco, quod in saeculo religionis admodum incurioso ortus is est qui, si quando librum sacra theologia refertum diuulgat, statim in linguas plurimas conuersus mille simul hominum in manibus uersatur, sicubi praelectiones habet, animos sescentos deuincit et fascinat. natus est in Heluetia, Romae institutioni sacerdotali se dedidit, anno tricesimo nondum exacto praecepta Caroli Barth tam subtiliter excussit ut aegre seniori persuaderet se tantulae aetatis tironem talem ac tantum scripsisse librum. triennio post professoris cathedram occupauit, mox alteri Concilio Vaticano consiliarii in partes adscitus nouum ecclesiae suae nasci ordinem auguratus est. deinceps dum scripta quasi e perenni fonte per annos amplius uiginti profundit famam penes academicos corroborauit, Christianorum corda beauit focillauit illuminauit. singularem uero habet hanc facultatem, sensus hominum atque mentes intellectu tam intimo percipiendi ut illi si qua palam proferre nesciant ipse oratione facunda resignet; quocirca fidei Catholicae addictis ecclesiam nouo patefactam lumine retexit, spem omnium ecclesiarum in unam denuo reducendarum reliquis adauxit. dicas auctorem controuersiarum, sane quod quaestiones maximi momenti, maximae item controuersiae tractare non reformidet. dicas ad radices molitorem uiae, qui hoc unum moliatur, ut Euangelium Christi omni fuco destitutum suis ipsum coloribus clarius lucescat. dicas rebellem, qui idcirco rebellet, quia fidei suae firmus propugnator est. dixerim equidem uirum hunc esse qui Beati Pauli edictum illud simplex et egregium, πάντα δοκιμάζετε, τὸ καλὸν κατέχετε, animo candido prosequatur.

Praesento uobis in Vniuersitate Tubingensi theologiae oecumenicae Professorem Ordinarium et Instituti studiis oecumenicis dediti Rectorem

IOHANNEM KÜNG

'AND *there appeared a great wonder.' Not least among the wonders of our irreligious age is a scholar whose numerous lengthy and learned works of theology have become best-sellers in many languages and whose lectures have held audiences of thousands enraptured in all parts of the globe. Born in Switzerland, educated for the priesthood in Rome, author at twenty-nine of a book on the teaching of Karl Barth which showed so profound an understanding of its subject that the elder theologian could scarcely believe that its author was a man so young; appointed professor of theology three years later, then consultant theologian to the Second Vatican Council, which he prayed would be the harbinger of a new era for his Church; thereafter, by his writings, issued in unbroken stream during more than twenty years, he has sealed his reputation in the eyes of scholars and gladdened and illumined the hearts of believers. He has that supreme gift of expressing clearly what others feel but cannot so well express; he has helped those of his own faith to see their Church in a clearer light and those of other faiths to look with fresh hope to the reunion of all Churches. Some call him controversial: but in his controversy is a deep engagement with the questions which most urgently confront mankind. Some call him radical: but in his radicalism is an unswerving desire to reach to the roots, to see the truth of the Gospel unclouded by false tradition. Some call him a rebel: but in his rebellion is the expression of his loyalty to his faith. I should say of him, rather, that he has taken as his watchword this precept of St Paul: 'Examine all things: hold fast that which is good.'[1]*

I present to you

HANS KÜNG,

Professor Ordinarius of Ecumenical Theology and Director of the Institute for Ecumenical Research, University of Tübingen.

[1] First Epistle to the Thessalonians, 5:21.

13

VIRO de re oeconomica tam praeclare, tam multifariam merito, praemii Nobeliani laureis ornato, quod nequit orator uester praeconio angusto et circumciso laudes deferre consentaneas, ipsum credo satisfactionem meam accepturum esse, ut qui magnum adsecutus sit nomen de Quod Nequit argumentando. sic enim argumentatione subtilissima disputauit: quod nequit, quae a plurimis comprobetur, rationalis electio consequi, si singulorum calculos subduxeris, idcirco quam probatissima rei publicae ratio reperiri nequit. quae conclusio, puto, certa est quia impossibilis est, tametsi nequitiam sapit. certe non oeconomicen tantum sed etiam politicen et philosophiam callentibus calcar admouit.

Num meministis Smithianum illud de caeca manu propositum? qui nempe praedicauit, si suis ipsorum commodis mercatores inseruirent, mercatoriae rationis aequilibritatem sponte sua nec manu factam maximum ciuitati commodum esse delaturam, rectoribus ciuitatis manum non uertentibus. quod propositum hic penitus explorauit, an ubique gentium uerum esse possit, adhibitis formularum mathematicarum ambagibus sane quam perplexis. rem in dubio reliquit, de uno tamen, ut opinor, non dubius, caecam manum plus semel ciuitatibus hodiernis caecum uulnus intulisse.

Oeconomices antistitem magis humanum, magis litteratum uix inuenias quam hunc uirum, qui quodlibet de fabulis Shakespearianis seu de fictilibus Sericis aenigma magistra mente soluat. ecastor, non minoris pedum agilitatis est homo quam cerebri: quadratae Salisubsaliorum choreae saepe fit particeps.

Fallor, an uaniloquentia mea stomachatus sagittarius noster soluta pharetra

legit in exitium spicula facta meum?[1]

properemus igitur uobis praesentare familiarem uestrum, Praelectorem olim Marshallianum, Collegii Churchilliani ter Socium Peregrinum, Academiae Britannicae hospitis iure Sodalem, in Vniuersitate Stanfordiana oeconomices et indagationis operariae Professorem,

CVNETIVM IOSEPHVM ARROW

[1] Ovid, *Amores*, 1. 1. 22.

IT is impossible, in a few words, to do justice to the many and varied achievements of our next guest, who is a Nobel prizewinner in economics. He will sympathise with my dilemma, for he knows all about impossibility. He made his name with the 'Arrow Impossibility Theorem', which is concerned with problems of 'social choice', and demonstrates, with symbolic logic, that we must despair of devising, by the simple calculation of the first, second, and third choices of individuals, a single combined preference ordering for society as a whole, and that it is therefore impossible, in principle, for any perfect form of government to exist – a Theorem (as Marvell nearly said) upon Impossibility, begotten by Despair, or (as Tertullian) certain because impossible. At all events, it has given rise to a vast literature, not only in economics but also in politics and philosophy.

He has also investigated the 'invisible hand' of Adam Smith: the concept that, if individuals selfishly pursue their private interests, market forces will spontaneously (as if by the operation of some invisible hand) ensure a state of equilibrium, productive of the maximum social good, without intervention by the hand of government. He has formulated, with complex mathematical arguments, the precise conditions which must be satisfied if the invisible hand is to work. Whether such conditions can ever be found in the real world, he leaves in doubt; but he would, I suspect, be the first to agree that in today's imperfect world the invisible hand is a visible failure.

He is the most learned and civilised economist you could hope to meet, and would win hands down at 'Mastermind' on any subject from Shakespeare to Chinese vases. And his feet are as nimble as his brain: he is an expert square-dancer.

But, lest further revelation of his versatility provoke him, like the god in Ovid's poem, to

> let fly an arrow with my name on it,

I hasten to present to you a man who has many friends among us (he once gave the Marshall Lectures, has three times been a Visiting Fellow of Churchill, and is a Corresponding Fellow of the British Academy),

KENNETH JOSEPH ARROW,

Professor of Economics and Operations Research, Stanford University.

PLASTICEN primus ab ipsa natura abstraxit artifex olim Graecus, qui nescioquem tam callide expressit ut non hominem ex aere fecisse diceretur sed iracundiam. ecce ille adest qui hanc artem usque adeo abstraxit unde ne transuersum quidem digitum ulterius abstrahi possit. mehercule Hephaestus, si capiti Iouis Mineruam parturienti partes obstetricias egit, quanto magis huic homini miracula sua elaboranti adfuisse putandus est, qui nec saxa sculpat nec lignum dolet neque aes fundat neque ex argilla fingat sed ferri frigidum horrorem compescat constringat contundat. quod inceptum non omnibus numeris statim perfectum atque absolutum enixus est: immo disciplinae mechanicae penes nos iam antea insudat, doctrinas de sculptura tralaticias et ediscit et edocet, archimagistro auscultat nec non auxiliatur Henrico Moore. uerum exacto tali tirocinio

> fit fragor: extemplo ruptis fornacibus Aetna
> eructat ferratam immani murmure molem,
> stricturas Chalybum et uectes et tigna metalli.
> hic simul ac terrae coniectus materiai
> decidit, insolitas elementa in disposituras
> singula quaeque abeunt nouaque in miracula currunt,
> clauorum rigidis compagibu' corpus in unum
> compacta aut liquido ferrumine conciliata:
> quorum haec praelustri rident fucata colore,
> illa incana situ, serrato dente, dehiscunt:
> nec resupina iacent neque recto uertice surgunt,
> uerum multiplici per humum reptare meatu
> aut suspendi auris, auris leuiora, uidentur.
> atque ea, natura cum sint et ab arte remota,
> propterea fit uti potius miremur eo quod
> singula membra quidem, si tantum singula lustres,
> muta sine ore tacent, brutae sine nomine massae,
> si tamen inspicias summam, quanam ratione
> singula sint membra et summa inter se uniter apta,
> percellit uisum atque animum insperata uoluptas.

Praesento uobis uirum in fabrica ferraria non tam χειρουργὸν quam χορηγόν, Imperii Britannici Commendatorem, Magistrum in Artibus, Collegii Christi alumnum et honoris causa Socium,

ANTONIVM ALVREDVM CARO

TO a Greek artist, who so successfully captured in bronze the character of his subject that he was said to have depicted 'not a person but passion personified',[1] may be ascribed the invention of abstract sculpture. If the process of abstraction has now reached its utmost limit, here is the man to whom credit is due. Hephaestus, patron god of metal-workers, assisted at the birth of Athena from the head of Zeus; and Hephaestus assuredly was present to deliver the brain-child of this man, who neither carves nor chisels nor casts nor moulds, in bronze, wood, stone, or clay, but tames the intransigent medium of steel and aluminium. Not that his brilliant new conception sprang forth, like Athena, fully armed. On the contrary, it was the product of long gestation – the Engineering Tripos, study and teaching in traditional sculptural modes, apprenticeship to the master, Henry Moore. Suddenly it was as if the Cyclopean forges deep inside Aetna had erupted in a gigantic explosion, spiralling into the air a cascade of metal bars and beams and girders and plates and rods and pipes, which tumbled to earth in miraculous new configurations, monumental constructions of welded and bolted steel, sometimes raw and rusty and jagged, sometimes enriched with a patina of vibrant colour, constructions which slither and snake their way across the ground, or seem to be suspended lighter than air, whose beauty consists in no likeness to nature or to art but in the visual and intellectual provocation of the relation of their elements to each other and to the whole, elements in isolation inert, anonymous, inexpressive, but together assuming a mute and magical eloquence.

I present to you a master choreographer in metal,

ANTHONY ALFRED CARO, C.B.E., M.A.,

Honorary Fellow of Christ's College.

---

[1] Pliny, *Natural History*, 34. 19. 82.

ADEST quem Ecclesiae dimidium suae paene nuncupes: tam huic intima cum ea intercedit necessitas, tam diuturna consuetudo. iam a teneris unguiculis cantorum gregi adscriptus est, mox donec bellum indictum est uespertino tintinnabulorum concentui intererat, custos idem et emendator horologii, postremo Virgarius amplius quinque abhinc lustris creatus est. Virgarius quis sit si quaeritis, eum scitote hoc nomine comprehendi qui pompae clericorum uirgam praeferat. et mehercule hic uir dum pompam cum uirga sua praegreditur, qua est auctoritate, qua dignitate natiua, neminem non admiratione perculsum relinquit. quin Sanctum Nicolaum nuper mentitus, quamquam tergo praegrauida munusculorum sarcina incuruato et capite cucullo et promissa barba obducto procedebat, processu tamen se plane pompatico prodidit.

Res omnibus nota: nescioquid restat quod uulgetur arcani. est subter adscensum in porticum meridionalem officina pusilla quidem sed omni instrumento referta. illic, si quando fistularum plumbo medendum est uel filis uim electricam ducentibus succurrendum uel Epei usus est arte lignaria, praestigiator hic noster extemporali quadam facilitate, quam in centuria fabrum forsitan adsecutus sit, dicto citius quod opus est absoluit: facta lux, fluit aqua, fixa compages, quod omnium praeter ipsius ac Dei spem fallit. illic militiae suae consilia capessit, illic copiarum calculos subducit: modo uestium uasorumque apparatum recenset, modo festis diebus supellectilem suam comparat, siue Christi natalibus pinorum proceritates instruendae siue Paschae sollemnibus narcissi ter centum exhibendi siue perfecta cantiuncularum festiuitate purgamenta cereorum mille sunt eliminanda.

Quae huius est antiquitatum cognitio, qui in rerum diuinarum obseruantia recti atque nefasti intellectus prope diuinus, permultis uicariis totidemque curionibus non apparitor tantum sed etiam admonitor adstitit: quos sane decet omnes (modo Horatii sint memores) una uoce Mercurium nostrum consalutare:

> tu pias laetis animas reponis
> sedibus uirgaque sacram coerces
> aurea turbam, superis deorum
> gratus et imis.[1]

Praesento uobis in Maiore Sanctae Mariae Ecclesia Virgarium

GEORGIVM ALBERTVM CLARKE

[1] Horace, *Odes*, 1. 10. 17–20.

BEFORE you stands a man whose life has been so interwoven with the University Church that to many he now seems to be a part of its fabric. He arrived as a choirboy at the age of nine, until war broke out he rang the curfew and wound the clock nightly, and he was appointed Verger more than a quarter of a century ago. Etymologists will tell you that a Verger is 'an official who carries a rod (verge) before the dignitaries of a Church or Cathedral'. And if you have seen him carry his verge, you will know that the authority and the natural dignity with which he leads the procession are a wonder and delight to behold. Indeed, though recently he was persuaded to walk up the aisle with his back bowed under a sack of Christmas presents and his face concealed by a hood and whiskers, nothing could disguise that stately processional pace.

That is the public side of his office: another side, half hidden, must also be revealed. Under the stairs to the South Gallery is a tiny, crowded workshop. Here, drawing perhaps on the skills which he learned in the Royal Army Ordnance Corps, whether the call is for carpentry, plumbing, or electric wiring, this master of improvisation will fix it, and it works, though only he and the Almighty know how. From these headquarters strategy is planned and resources are marshalled – the provision and good order of plate and vestments, the special requirements of festal occasions, whether Christmas trees twenty feet high, or three hundred daffodils on Easter Day, or the clearing of a thousand candles after a festival of carols.

With his encyclopaedic knowledge of the history and traditions of the Church, and his uncompromising instinct for what is right and proper, he has been the mentor of a long line of Vicars and Curates, who will all (if they remember their Horace) hymn with one voice this Mercury of Great St Mary's:

> O thou that dost the pious souls
> Guide with thy golden rod,
> A faithful Clarke to clerks below
> And upon high to God.

I present to you

GEORGE ALBERT CLARKE,

Verger of Great St Mary's Church.

O MNIA mors claudit: sed donec uita supersit,
    temptandum est aliquod non parui nominis actum.

Erat olim in nosocomio iuuenis operata, quae artem medicinalem perspexit quantum sub mortis aduentum claudicare et uacillare uideretur neque supremum diem obituris amplius subsidii ualeret uel doloris leuamen adferre. haec autem, quae aegrotantes propter singularem patientiam et auscultandi facultatem in tam perfectam familiaritatem adducere calleret ut intimos angores ultro resignare uellent, infando illi et omnium communi mortis timori comminus ire condiscebat. nempe sub ipsam mortem sciebat modo mutuum nasci posse amorem, modo magnum absconditae nobilitatis elucere documentum:

nam uerae uoces tum demum pectore ab imo
eliciuntur et eripitur persona, manet res,

sicut Lucretius dixit. ergo, ut erat animo indefesso et propositi tenacissima, aliquando in medicorum classem adscripta hospitium morbo insanabili laborantibus fundare destinauit, si forte mortis tenebras scintilla lucis illuminaret neue, quem spes defecisset sanitatis, is omni simul copia caritatis indigeret. illic disciplinam medicamentariam fidei Christianae lumine consociatam et corroboratam exhibens, noua morientibus dolorum lenimina, noua cognatis aegrimoniarum solamina repperit, quae postmodo in hospitiis et ualetudinariis cum domi tum peregre reliqua medicorum gens amplecti consueuit nec non penes nos etiam Cantabrigienses Domicilii nomine Arturi Rank uocati curatores libenter adsciscunt.

'Quae latebra est' interrogauit Seneca 'in quam non intret metus mortis? quae tam emunita et in altum subducta uitae quies, quam non dolor territet?' adstat quae interroganti responsum suo iure reddat.

Praesento uobis Excellentissimi Ordinis Imperii Britannici Dominam Commendatricem, Sancti Christophori apud Sydenhamenses Hospitii Moderatricem,

CAECILIAM SAUNDERS

D EATH *closes all; but something ere the end,*
Some work of noble note may yet be done.[1]

Many years ago a young nurse observed how the noble struggle to cure illness faltered at the approach of death and could find then no further resource to supply the needs and comfort the pains of the terminally ill. Through her unique capacity for listening to the sick and enabling them to speak of their inner pain, by her gift for making an intimate friendship with the dying, she learned how to meet and engage with that great unspoken fear which haunts mankind, the fear of death. She knew that, in the face of death, love may flow from the heart of comforter and comforted alike, and that here above all a hidden nobility may find its true expression. 'In the last scene between ourselves and death,' said Montaigne, 'there is no more pretence. We cannot but display such goodness and purity as lies at the bottom our soul.'[2] With singular strength of will she enrolled in the ranks of the physicians, and conceived, designed, and created a hospice for the dying, to bring care where there is no cure, and to show that in the shadow of death there may be light. Uniting the skills of medicine with the illumination of her religious faith, she pioneered new methods in the control of pain and the comforting of the bereaved, which have been adopted the world over, in a multitude of hospices and other centres of care; and Cambridge is proud to have one of these, in which her methods are followed, known as Arthur Rank House.

'What place is there,' asked the philosopher, 'where fear of death does not enter? What place so peaceful and secure that pain brings no terror?'[3] Here is one who has found an answer.

I present to you

Dame CICELY SAUNDERS,

Chairman, St Christopher's Hospice, Sydenham.

[1] Tennyson, *Ulysses*, 51–2.
[2] *Essays*, I. 19. Montaigne is echoing Lucretius 3. 57–8, which is quoted in the Latin speech.
[3] Seneca, *Epistulae Morales*, 82. 4.

A RMIS Achilleis Hephaestus ultimam impositurus manum caelamen hoc extudit,

ποταμοῖο μέγα σθένος Ὠκεανοῖο
ἄντυγα πὰρ πυμάτην σάκεος πύκα ποιητοῖο,[1]

nimirum quod secundum priscam doctrinam planum mortales habitare orbem fingebat Oceano ambitum circumuago. quamquam hunc errorem iam dudum exsibilauimus, tamen in magnorum marium motibus nonnulla manent mysteria, quorum summus nunc incedit interpres et mystagogus. primum sollertiae suae specimen saeuiente bello ostendit, cum classibus nostris oram Africae septentrionalem mox occupaturis praedixit quae uno quoque die fluctuum altitudines enauigandae forent. postea immensum maris spatium quod a Noua Zelandia usque ad Alaskam patescit stationibus speculatoriis instruxit, idcirco ut hypothesin suam argumentis comprobaret, eas quae litora Californiensia uerberent undas immane quantum aequoris esse permensas, tempestatibus scilicet hibernis in hemisphaerio australi iam pridem suscitatas. ad terram paulisper adpulsus librum de orbis rotatione conscripsit. meministis fortasse Ducissam Aliciae fabulantem:

si quisque res agat suas nec alienas moretur,
ecastor festinantius rotetur summa rerum.

at haec mera somnia. nam *mundi claudicat axis*, ut ait Lucretius,[2] neque constanti celeritate circumfertur orbis. res bene nota, quaestio diu tractata, solutio ab hoc profecta, qui quid pontus, quid terra, quid aer ad has uicissitudines progignendas conferant uno simul obtutu comprehendit. addas quod nouam fluctuum reciprocorum diuinationem inuenit *prouidus aestuspex*, et *qua ui maria alta tumescant*[3] auritis machinamentis sciscitatus est. sed quid plura? unum adicere sufficit, quo planius uniuersam collegarum adprobationem colligatis: dux est et signifer, qui nouas inuestigationum areas identidem designauit designatasque explorandi ardore sectatores concussit plurimos.

Praesento uobis Regiae Societatis externo iure Sodalem, aureo nomismate a Regia Astronomicorum Sodalitate donatum, Collegii Churchilliani hospitis iure bis Socium, Geophysices in Vniuersitate Californiensi ad sinum Sancti Didaci Professorem,

WALTERVM HENRICVM MUNK

[1] Homer, *Iliad*, 18. 607–8.
[2] Lucretius, 6. 1107.
[3] Horace, *Odes*, 3. 27. 8, Vergil, *Georgics*, 2. 479.

W HEN *Hephaestus forged new armour for Achilles, his final touch was to emboss*

> *The mighty Ocean's ever-flowing stream*
> *Around the circling rim of the great shield.*

In so doing, he was reflecting the ancient world-view, of a flat earth surrounded by a solitary Ocean. Today we know better. And yet the movements of the mighty oceans still hold their mysteries, and no one has done more to fathom those mysteries than our next honorand. He gave a foretaste of his skill in the war, when he worked out a method for predicting, days ahead, the height of waves due to break on the beaches chosen for the invasion of North Africa. Later he established a network of wave-stations along a vast arc from New Zealand to Alaska, and so proved the rightness of his theory that the swell which rolls onto the beaches of California has its origin 5,000 miles away in the wintry storms of the southern hemisphere. Returning for a while to terra firma, *he wrote a book on* The Rotation of the Earth. *'If everyone minded their own business', said the Duchess to Alice, 'the world would go round a deal faster.' In fact, as has long been known, the earth wobbles on its axis and does not rotate at a constant speed. He put the study of this old problem on a new footing by giving the first unified account of the manifold phenomena of sea, land, and air which contribute to these variations. He has also developed new techniques of tidal prediction, he has traced the dynamics of waves with acoustical scanners – but a list of his many activities will not adequately explain why his colleagues hold him in such high esteem. It is, above all, because he is a pioneer, who has constantly identified new fields of inquiry where progress may be made, and has inspired countless others to follow the leads which he has given.*

I present to you a Foreign Member of the Royal Society, gold medallist of the Royal Astronomical Society, twice Overseas Fellow of Churchill College,

WALTER HEINRICH MUNK,

Professor of Geophysics, University of California at San Diego.

CAMVS Camenam concelebrat suam,
etsi paterni te genius loci
   septentrionali sub axe
      contigerat grauiore thyrso,

qua bruta tellus imbribus ingemit
supraque uallem nubibus hispidam
   mensem per Aprilem canora
      barbiton emodulatur ales,

o laureati carminis artifex,
siue aestuoso buculam anhelitu
   dumeta texentem togamue
      excutientem anatem gelatam

siue enatantem tegmine frondium
electrinarum concinis anthiam
   noctemue ni latrent quietam
      rauca canes crepitentque mulctra.

te fabulosas historias iuuat
componere: a te larua renascitur
   siluestris et morosa cornix
      et genus Iapeti solutum

numquam catena, numquam adamantino
angore: te non belua, non homo
   fallit neque humanis sepulta
      pectoribus rabies ferina.

tu liberasti scilicet intimo
sermone uoces longius abditas,
   quae sorte mortali carentes
      omne sequens resonent in aeuum.

Praesento uobis carminum non prius auditorum cantorem, Musarum sacerdotem omnibus bonarum litterarum cultoribus acceptissimum, Magistrum in Artibus, Collegii Pembrochiani alumnum et honoris causa Socium, Excellentissimo Ordini Imperii Britannici adscriptum, priuilegio reginali nuper laurea donatum Apollinari, quem laureis etiam nostris coronare dulce est et decorum,

EDVARDVM IACOBVM HUGHES

A heartfelt welcome to our Poet Laureate! We are proud to salute you as our own, for you did once muse by the banks of the Cam, though the strongest inspiration you found in the Yorkshire moorland of your birth,

where the howlings of heaven pour down onto earth,

and

curlews in April hang their harps over the misty valleys.

You tell of nature in all her variety, of the cows

looping the hedges with their warm wreaths of breath,

of

the wild duck shaking off her Arctic swaddling,

of the pike

in an amber cavern of weeds,

and

a cool small evening shrunk to a dog bark and the clank of a bucket.

You are a maker of myths: you have brought back to life macabre Wodwo, fretful Crow, Prometheus

waking in a new aeon to the old chains and the old agony.

You know both man and beast, and see the violence of nature deep in the human soul. You have freed from the language images long awaiting release, which, now released, will live for centuries to come.

I present to you a bold and original poet, of the widest popular appeal, so that we may crown him with laurels of our own,

EDWARD JAMES HUGHES, O.B.E., M.A.,

Honorary Fellow of Pembroke College, Poet Laureate.

SOCRATEM adsector aliquis per iocum concauo adsimulauit sigillo, cuius in secessu interiore reconditas deorum imagunculas deprehendas: autumauit uidelicet, cum Socratem introspexisses, aureos diuinos admirandos adparere thesauros. in mentem mihi subuenit haec similitudo cum hospitis qui agmen cogit Studia Platonica nuper euolui et introspexi: quo in uolumine continetur pars magna commentariorum quibus Platonis doctrinas tot per annos tam luculente explanauit ut omnium qui ubique terrarum antiquae philosophiae studiis incumbunt agnoscatur ipse coryphaeus. philosophus autem an philologus appelletur parum interest, ut qui ingenio uersatili modo sapientiae contemplatiuae excelsa conscendat, modo perplexi sermonis ambages et arcana perscrutetur. dum a Platone suo otiatur, quis huius curis campus non patescit? nam ab Anaxagora ad Epicurum facili pede transcurrit, neque ei minus cordi est institutionis Graecorum ciuilis cognitio quam religionis medicinae mathematices inuestigatio. iam diu Socratis historiam conscribit, qua hominem multiplicem uerius quam antea cuiquam contigerit eum explicaturum esse omnes augurantur. cuius historiae primitias nuper cum nobis beneuole communicauit, dum apud Collegium Christi totum annum Socii Peregrini iure consumit. et animis quam gratis uirum uenerandum doctrinas suas expromentem, responsa nostra exposcentem, senioribus iunioribusque colloquiis priuatis et publicis semper uacantem, a quibus nemo non animo confirmatus et scientia instructus locupletiore discessit, alterum Socratem ab Elysio rediuiuum, uidimus audiuimus dileximus.

Praesento uobis Academiae Britannicae hospitis iure Socium, in Vniuersitate Princetonensi Philosophiae Professorem emeritum,

GREGORIVM VLASTOS

O NE *of the more playful disciples of Socrates likened him to a type of hollow statuette which, when opened up, is found to contain little figures of gods inside; for (he claimed) when you look inside Socrates, divine and golden and marvellous treasures are revealed.[1] This image came into my mind as I opened and looked into the* Platonic Studies *of our final guest, a collection of many of the essays with which he has, over the years, so brilliantly elucidated Plato's thought and established for himself a reputation as the foremost student of ancient philosophy in the world. In them he shows a rare ability to range between the extremes of, on the one hand, abstract and imaginative philosophical analysis and, on the other, the scrupulous examination of linguistic minutiae; and never have the skills of the philosopher and the philologist been more happily combined in one man. But do not suppose that Plato is his only interest. From Anaxagoras to Epicurus he roams with equal sureness of step, and the political institutions of Greece concern him no less than its religion and medicine and mathematics. He is currently writing a book on Socrates, and all know that it will be a landmark in the centuries-old endeavour to come to terms with this challenging figure. He recently did us the honour of spending a year among us, as Distinguished Visiting Fellow of Christ's College. And to all, junior and senior alike, who saw and heard this legendary man expounding and testing his ideas, available at all times to all, for public or private discussion, from which they could not but emerge uplifted in spirit and enriched in learning, it must have seemed that Socrates himself trod the earth once more.*

I present to you

GREGORY VLASTOS,

Corresponding Fellow of the British Academy, formerly Stuart Professor of Philosophy, Princeton University.

[1] Plato, *Symposium*, 215.

SVNT in Africae secessu fauces Olduuaianae: quae quo casu repertae sint operae pretium est cognoscere. olim retiarius quidam Monacensis, tam papilionibus intentus quam sui immemor, desuper paene incidit. o casum peropportunum! nam ossa iamdudum sepulta nec non quadrupedis tripollicalis dentes detegit detectaque Caesari reportat. Caesar spectaculo obstupet uirumque inter geologos primarium ire exploratum iubet. sed bellum mox indictum, explorationibus supersessum est. confecto tandem bello fossae deprimuntur ductu atque auspicio uiri inter clarissimos alumnorum nostrorum numerandi, Ludouici Leakey, marita maritum primo adiuuante, defuncti in officium inde suffecta.

O claro marito marita uel clarior! quot quantaque in ualle ossiculorum referta effodit miracula! en simius Saturno iam rege exoletus, cui nomen est inditum Proconsul Africanus. en pedum uestigia cineri Volcanio impressa, unde illud iam compertum habemus, quod deus pithecanthropo abhinc amplius triciens centenis milibus annorum

> os sublime dedit caelumque uidere
> iussit et erectos in sidera tollere uultus.[1]

en Homunculi Nucifrangibuli caluaria, malis immanibus, molaribus giganteis dehiscentis, quem quiuis hominum sapientiorum, Enniani uersiculi memor

> simia quam similis, turpissima bestia, nobis,[2]

longinqua cognatione non directo limite nobis esse coniunctum gratuletur.

Quicumque huius libros euoluit non ossa tantum et lapides legit. legit etiam inuia terrarum, itinerum pericula, aquarum inopias, morbos febriculosos, monstra formicarum, incursus leonum et semibarbarorum. sed legit in primis inuicto et indefesso animo mulierem, quae Darwinii nostri sententiam, in Africa natum esse hominem primigenium, omnibus fere comprobauit, et lineam antecessorum nostrorum in paene infinitam anteacti temporis aetatem prosecuta est.

Praesento uobis Academiae Britannicae Sociam, faucium Olduuaianarum explorationibus praefectam,

MARIAM DOUGLAS LEAKEY

[1] Ovid, *Metamorphoses*, 1. 85–6.
[2] Ennius, *Satires*, 69 Vahlen.

THERE is a gorge in East Africa called Olduvai. It was discovered by accident, when an absent-minded Professor from Munich with a butterfly net nearly fell over the side. He took home fossils and the teeth of a three-toed horse. The Kaiser commanded his leading geologist to set forth. But war intervened, and excavations were suspended. When they were resumed, they were led by a man whom we are proud to number among our most distinguished alumni, the late Louis Leakey, whose work was aided and is even now continued by his no less distinguished wife.

What wonders she found, when set down, like the prophet Ezekiel, in the midst of the valley which was full of bones! Proconsul Africanus, an ape twenty million years old; footprints preserved in volcanic ash, proof that as long as three and a half million years ago ape-man walked not on all fours but

> God lifted up his face and bade him see
> The sky and raise his eyes toward the stars;

and the skull of Nutcracker Man, with enormous jaws and gigantic molars – and if you remember the poet Ennius,

> The ape, which has an ugly face,
> Is brother to the human race,

you will be grateful that this species is only a distant cousin.

Hers is a story not only of bones and stones but also of courage and adventure: trackless terrain and perilous journeys; shortage of water and tropical diseases; giant ants, marauding lions, and hostile tribesmen. It is thanks in large part to her discoveries and her writings that Africa is now seen to be, as Darwin predicted, the probable birthplace of man, and that the line of the ancestors of Adam has been traced into a past unimaginably remote.

I present to you

MARY DOUGLAS LEAKEY, F.B.A.,

Director of the Olduvai Gorge Excavation.

INSEQVITVR omnis Mineruae uir, in artibus tam campestribus quam umbraticis, in negotiis tam saecularibus quam clericis expeditus, qui, dum litteris operam insumit gloriosam, summa tractauit Academiae munia, summa Ciuitatis.

> Hunc chori partem pede qui manuque
> ludit hostiles iuuenum cateruas,
> hunc chori regem meminere campi
> Twickenhamenses.

quodsi subcaerulam uestem laena mox atriore commutauit, iuuenalem pariter cum ueste non deposuit ardorem, quippe cui quindecumanorum nostrorum Praesidis officio fungi diuturno placeret. huius cum nomine uinculo sempiterno copulabitur Collegium Selwynianum, cui nouas in fortunas renascenti septem et uiginti per annos Magister, ne dicam architectus, adfuit. uidimus Historiae Ecclesiasticae Professorem Dixianum, uidimus Aeui Recentioris Historiae Professorem Regium, uidimus Procancellarii dignitatem exporrecta fronte sustinentem, Horatiani praecepti 'aequam rebus in arduis seruare mentem' semper tenacem. et quid quod extra fines Academiae longe huius fama processit? nonne ab Archiepiscopis praedicto arbitrorum consessui praefectus est? nonne Academiae Britannicae Socii quondam Praesidem, Academiae suae nuper Cancellarium Noruicenses creauerunt? uirum miramur in omnia uersatilem, scriptorem laudamus fecundi pectoris. nempe si quem argumenta filo deducta ampliore delectant, de Ecclesia Reformata commentarium contexuit nec non de Ecclesia Victoriana par nobile librorum. sin singulorum uitae hominum et ingenia libentius leguntur, Iohannem Henricum Oxoniensem enarrauit, Oxoniensium a fide Anglica desciscentium animas examinauit. sin magis sunt cordi res artioribus circumscriptae terminis, adest palmaris ille et omnium leporum differtus libellus, in quo caelatoris more insculpantis anulo sigillum describit quid olim in paroecia rusticana – pro tempus irreparabile, pro mores inuersi – inter pastorem dominumque intercedere soleret commercii. profecto in tali argumentorum diuersitate in uno sibi consentit, quod nihil umquam scripsit, nihil dixit, nihil denique fecit quin ex animo ingenuo et candido omnibus numeris perfectum atque perpolitum profluxerit.

Praesento uobis uirum reuerendum, Ordini insigniter meritorum adscriptum, Excellentissimi Ordinis Imperii Britannici Equitem Commendatorem, Sacrae Theologiae Doctorem, Collegiorum Diui Iohannis Euangelistae et Wolfsoniani nec non Aulae Sanctae Trinitatis honoris causa Socium,

GVLIELMVM ODOENVM CHADWICK

NEXT *comes a man of infinite variety, scholar and sportsman, priest and man of affairs, who in a life of the highest academic distinction has attained the highest offices which the University can propose and the highest honours which the State can bestow.*

> *Upon the field of Twickenham*
> *His glory first was seen,*
> *As member twice, then captain*
> *Of the Varsity XV.*

And if thereafter he shed the shirt of light blue for the darker hue of cassock and gown, he never shed his youthful passion, for he served for many years as President of our Rugby Club. His name will for ever be linked with Selwyn College, of which he was Master for twenty-seven years, and architect of its modern fortunes. The University saw him in turn as Dixie Professor of Ecclesiastical History and Regius Professor of Modern History, and as Vice-Chancellor, a rôle which he sustained with calm and dignity at our most troubled time, keeping his head when all about were losing theirs. The world at large saw him as Chairman of the Archbishops' Commission on Church and State and as President of the British Academy, and sees him now as Chancellor of the University of East Anglia. And if we marvel at the manifold transformations and limitless energy of the man, no less do we marvel at the multitude and diversity of his writings. If we like our history painted on a broader canvas, we turn to The Reformation *or the two great volumes on* The Victorian Church. *If we prefer the history of ideas and the personalities which gave birth to them, he has explored the life of John Henry Newman and* The Mind of the Oxford Movement. *Or if our taste is for history intimate and parochial, there is* Victorian Miniature, *in which, like a master craftsman inscribing a gem within the bezel of a ring, he depicts an irrecoverable world of parson and squire. In the midst of such diversity one talent remains constant: the consummate style, the graceful and effortless ease which have informed his every word and action.*

I present to you

The Reverend WILLIAM OWEN CHADWICK,
O.M., K.B.E., D.D., F.B.A.,

Honorary Fellow of St John's and Wolfson Colleges and of Trinity Hall.

'SIQVANDO non satis ualent uerba' dixit Claudius ille Franco-gallorum 'est opus musices.' quo igitur uerborum praeconio Poloniae hunc filium praedicem, qui melodias natiuas Polyhymnia Europaea tam mirum in modum condiit ut artifex euaderet indolis unicae, in auia Pieridum loca semper auditorem prouocans? hic, ne post silentium a patriae praedonibus odeis indictum omne conciuibus deesset solatium, opera priorum clauiculis eburneis accommodauit et suis ipse digitis in Varsauiensibus exprompsit popinis. cuius industriae superest documentum illud egregium, Paganiniana multifariis uariata coloribus Cantilena. mox altero in alterius locum suffecto tyranno, ita ut Symphonia Prima tamquam communi noxia saluti proscriberetur, obmutescere maluit quam praua iubentibus concedere. restituta demum libertate uox cum in patriam tum per attonita Europae auditoria excessit euasit erupit. Neniam Belae Bartok in honorem compositam patria salutauit, Italia Ludorum Veneticorum ardore incensa exsultauit, at nosmet ipsi omnium primi audiuimus Aldeburgii Telam Verborum quam diuina Petri nostratis uoce decantandam contexuit, audiuimus Londinii Concentum qui ab organo tetrachordo Mstislauae Rostropovich grauiter sonante reboauit. accedit quod operum suorum eximius est e tribunali interpres, qui nouo ἐνθουσιασμῷ atque adeo ἔρωτι correptos uel lenissimo baculi sui motu musicos reddat.

Nuper summo patriae nostrae praemio, Regiae Philharmonicorum Societatis aureo nomismate, ornatus est. nos uel impensius honoribus nostris hunc iuuat ornare, qui ipse honore praecipuo has nostras caerimonias ornauerit: cuius quippe curis nouissimis prouisum est ut pompa sollemnis in Senaculum incederet tuba tonitru tremendo tara-tantara tonante.

Praesento uobis

WITOLD LUTOSŁAWSKI

32

'**M**USIC *begins' said Debussy 'where the words fail.' Then how can words of mine describe the achievement of this son of Poland, who has blended his native inheritance with the innovations of the West, to create music of a character unique and individual, ever reaching forward into new realms of sound? As a young man, when the concert halls were silenced by his country's oppressors, he gave cheer to his countrymen by adapting for piano the composers of the past; and from such origins arose the dazzling* Variations on a Theme of Paganini, *first performed by his own hands in the cafés of Warsaw. When one tyrant gave way to another, he saw his* First Symphony *banned as decadent. But, when freedom returned, his genius, long nurtured in solitude, burst forth upon an astonished and enraptured Europe. If his homeland first saluted the* Funeral Music, *dedicated to the memory of Bartók, and Italy acclaimed the* Venetian Games, *it was we who were privileged to be first hearers of the web of words* (Paroles Tissées) *which he wove for Peter Pears to sing at Aldeburgh, and the* Cello Concerto *performed in London by Mstislav Rostropovich. He is not only a composer but also a matchless interpreter of his own works, and to his presence on the rostrum, calm yet magnetic, his players respond with a new spontaneity,* con spirito *and* con amore.

Last year he received our country's highest musical honour, the Gold Medal of the Royal Philharmonic Society. Today he has honoured us, even as we honour him: for his latest work, composed for this ceremony, is the glorious fanfare which accompanied our procession.

I present to you

WITOLD LUTOSŁAWSKI

IBAT forte sacro uir de grege, collis ubi alto
tramite consurgit Turrim prope Londiniensem.
nescioquis sedet in muro: prior ille sedentem
occupat: 'Heus, bone, dic sodes: quo contio fiat,
quid faciam? orator fieri uolo.' 'Eia, ere, murum
conscendas, complode manus: mihi crede, Quirites
concurrent.' scandit, plaudit, concurritur: euge!

At qui concursus, quae concursuum diuturnitas! nam Mercuri diebus
ad Turrim, quot Sabbatis ad tribunal in Angulo Oratorum positum
concurritur. ibi iustum et tenacem propositi uirum non uulgi uox
reclamitantis mente quatit solida, non auream uerborum compescit
copiam: quin integritate animi atque aequitate uel nullius fidei homines
deuincit mirabundosque dimittit. nec pulpita tantum sub diuo col-
locauit, sed annos amplius quadraginta Aulae a Via Regia cognominatae
praefuit. hunc maximo sua adfecit honore Ecclesia, quem summi
Methodistarum conuenticuli Praesidem elegerit, inaudito Respublica,
quem primum clericorum fidei addictorum non Anglicanae in Procerum
Domum euexerit. nimirum non unius est hic Ecclesiae, sed uniuersae;
nec, dum uerba peruulgat Dei, res tangere auersatur saeculares,
causarum optimarum licet publici consili auctoribus inuisarum uindex
strenuus. nonne uero Iohannis illius, qui Euangelium circum pagos et
compita disseminauit, germanus est filius, qui libros exarando,
commentariola diurna publicando, uocem aethere diffusili didendo,
mare terram aera permetiendo ipse in fabulam euaserit, totius nationis
corda atque adeo conscientiam mouerit?

Praesento uobis uirum reuerendum et admodum honorabilem,
Magistrum in Artibus, Collegii Sanctae Catharinae Virginis alumnum et
honoris causa Socium,

DONALDVM OLIVERVM Baronem SOPER

ONCE *upon a time a young Methodist minister, not long down from Cambridge, arrived on Tower Hill and found a man sitting on a wall. 'How do you start a meeting?' he asked. 'Get up on the wall, Guv'nor, and clap yer 'ands; they'll come.' He got up, and clapped, and they came – and for more than fifty years they came, to the wall on Tower Hill on Wednesdays, and on Sundays to the soapbox at Speakers' Corner in Hyde Park. Hobgoblin nor heckler could daunt his courage, or silence the flow of his oratory, and even those of little faith admired and cheered the manifest integrity and nobility of his purpose. He set up an indoor pulpit too, as Superintendent for forty years of the West London Mission in Kingsway Hall. He received the highest honour which his Church can bestow, the Presidency of the Methodist Conference, and an unparalleled distinction of State, the first minister outside the established Church to enter the House of Lords. His ministry is wider than any Church and engages with the temporal no less than the spiritual, and does not shun the unpopular fight. As the true heir to John Wesley, who carried his message into the streets and marketplaces and into every corner of the land, so he, by his books, his journalism, his broadcasts and his travels, has become a living legend, and has touched the hearts and minds and stirred the conscience of a whole nation.*

I present to you the Reverend and Right Honourable

DONALD OLIVER Baron SOPER, M.A.,

Honorary Fellow of St Catharine's College.

S ENATOR quidam aqua et igni interdictus, cum ad professionem
rhetorices confugisset, de Fortunae ludibrio conquerebatur, quod e
senatoribus faceret professores, e professoribus senatores. Fortunae
cum hospita hac proxima commercium nemo nostrum indignabitur:
quae Gulielmi illius Spooner, Collegii Noui Custodis, e filia nata neptis,
postquam famae primitias in Aula Dominae Margarethae adsecuta est,
ad Londinienses, Sheffieldienses, denique Girtonenses auecta chemiam
docendo se dedidit. tum, puto, aurem dea uellit et 'Quidni' admonet

> 'iuuat integros accedere fontes
> atque haurire iuuatque nouos decerpere flores
> haerentemque tuo capiti petere inde coronam
> unde prius nulli uelarunt tempora Musae'?

quo admonitu confirmata ad Aulam Nouam transiit, cuius adsistebat
incunabulis et in iustam Collegii magnitudinem adolescentis prima
omnium Praeses creata est. quid mirum si mulier patre praefecto classis
orta et inter puellas quondam uersata nauticula*rens*es hoc tantum
officium sollertia uelut hereditaria gubernabat? adde quod nullo
quamuis uulgari opificio se maiorem habebat: namque si hortulis, si
plumbo fistularum, si filis uim electricam ducentibus prouidendum, si
tegumenta librorum resarcienda, siue Epei erat usus arte lignaria, dicto
citius ipsa Praeses praesto adest. dignissimam demum hanc iudicauimus
cui committeretur nulli antehac mulieri commissa dignitas, totius
Academiae gubernatio. quam firma manu rem summam procurauerit,
quantam maiestatem quali uenustate condiendo caerimoniis nostris
praesederit uidistis omnes. mehercule contemplanti mihi quantum pro
institutione feminarum nostratium nuper profecerimus (cuius haec ipsa
profectus pars fuit magna) sponte sua surgit in ora immortale illud
Euripidis canticum, nouae compos ueritatis:

> nunc uatum seriem Musa uetat male
> de uirtute mea dicere masculam:
> tandem pars sua laudis
> genti femineae uenit.

Praesento uobis, ut nouum coronae decerpat florem, Excellentissimi
Ordinis Imperii Britannici Dominam Commendatricem, Magistram in
Artibus, Aulae Nouae et Collegiorum Girtonensis et Robinsoniani
honoris causa Sociam,

ALICIAM ROSEMARIAM MURRAY

AN exiled Roman Senator, obliged to turn his hand to the teaching of oratory, complained that through the caprice of Fortune administrators were being transformed into professors, and professors into administrators.[1] We have no complaint with the transformation which Fortune had in store for the career of our next honorand. The granddaughter of Warden Spooner of New College, she won academic distinction at Lady Margaret Hall and became a lecturer in chemistry at London, Sheffield, and finally at Girton. But then she chose to

> Approach and drink untasted springs
> And pluck new flowers, and for her head
> Gather a glorious coronal
> From places where the Muses never
> Had wreathed another's brow.[2]

She became the first Tutor of New Hall, and then, as the foundation grew into a College, she was appointed its first President. The skill of her captaincy surprised no one: she was an Admiral's daughter and had served as an officer in the Wrens. But she also excelled in skills less august: for she delighted to combine with the office of President the rôles of gardener, carpenter, plumber, electrician, and binder of books. We invited her to take the helm of the whole University, as our first woman Vice-Chancellor. With what sureness of control she managed our affairs you all know; with what dignity she presided over our ceremonies you all have seen. As I survey what women have achieved in our University during recent years, and her signal part in promoting these achievements, the prophetic words of Euripides spring unprompted to my lips, charged with a new conviction:

> Bards shall strike up a newer story,
> And myths of old shall fade:
> To woman comes her share of glory,
> And honour that is due shall now be paid.[3]

So that she may add one more flower to her coronal, I present to you

Dame ALICE ROSEMARY MURRAY, M.A.,

Honorary Fellow of New Hall, and of Girton and Robinson Colleges.

[1] Pliny, *Epistles*, 4. 11.
[2] Lucretius, 1. 927–30.
[3] Euripides, *Medea*, 415–20.

INTER Britannos et Americanos, dixit quispiam, claustrum interponit impenetrabile non tam aequor Atlanticum quam linguae communis non communis usus. quo magis iuuat hospitem utriusque linguae sermones doctum salutare, qui decem iam lustra internunti partes ita sustinet, nobis quidem Americanum nonnihil sonans, illis elocutionis exemplar Britannicae, ut cum linguae tum Oceani dissociabilis claustra perfringat. recte uero Horatius, caelum mutare qui trans mare currant, non animum. hic certe animum non mutauit Britannicum, huius dicta Britannica tamquam moneta percussa ueri nomismatis instar tinniunt. at quem sibi uindicat Britannia Britannicum, nos nobismet ipsi Cantabrigienses Cantabrigiensem uindicamus. hunc uidimus litterarum Anglicarum discipulum primarium, mimici Mummorum gregis conditorem, libelli qui Granta inscribitur editorem, hunc audiuimus hac ipsa in curia praelectoris Rediani nomine oratorem catum concinnum copiosum. quo ergo potissimum tollatur praeconio? num rerum diurnarum laudemus fabulatorem, Custodis nostri quinque et uiginti per annos a commentariis? an Clius famulum, qui quinque saeculorum annales conscripserit, enarrauerit, sua ipsius persona in scaenam induxerit? immo laudamus in primis noui epistularum commerci repertorem, quod cum uno quoque nostrum iam quadraginta exercet annos, quippe qui epistulis bis mille conscriptis modo rerum quibus ipse intersit euentus explicet, modo anthropologi ritu mores suorum nobis admodum alienos edisserat, ut quidquid agant homines Americani, quae eorum sint uota, qui timores, quae gaudia, qui discursus, certa perspectum ratione teneamus.

Praesento uobis inter Excellentissimi Ordinis Imperii Britannici Equites Commendatores honoris causa adscriptum, Baccalaureum in Artibus, Collegii Iesu alumnum et honoris causa Socium,

ALFREDVM ALISTAIR COOKE

S OMEONE *has said that the greatest barrier between the English and the Americans is not the Atlantic Ocean but their common language. Here is a man who has broken down that barrier, whose distinctive voice, a little American to us, more than a little British to them, has been heard on both sides of the Atlantic for half a century: the unofficial ambassador of two continents.*

He has proved the truth of Horace's maxim, that

> *Those who go across the sea*
> *Change the sky but not their hearts.*[1]

At heart he remains an Englishman, and his words ring like the true coin of the realm. But he is more than an Englishman: he is a Cambridge man, who took a First in the English Tripos, founded the Mummers, and edited Granta. *And he is no stranger to this Senate-House: for he once beguiled us here with the wit and wisdom of his Rede Lecture* (The American in England: Emerson to S.J.Perelman, *1975*). *We praise him as a journalist: for twenty-five years author of a daily dispatch to* The Guardian. *We praise him as a historian: who wrote, narrated, and enacted before our eyes the annals of five centuries* (America: A Personal View, *BBC TV, 1972*). *But we praise him above all as the inventor of a new art of communication: who, week by week for forty years, in letters now numbering more than two thousand, delivered to every household in the land, sometimes, as an eye-witness, catching history on the wing, sometimes, like an anthropologist, cataloguing the strange manners of his adopted people, has told us how life is lived in America.*

I present to you

ALFRED ALISTAIR COOKE, HON. K.B.E., B.A.,

Honorary Fellow of Jesus College.

---

[1] Horace, *Epistles*, 1. 11. 27.

AGMEN claudit mulier statuaria, quae dum hominum auium ferarum naturam ex aere fundit unicae uirtutis indolem praestat. haec enim animantium subter superficiem tam penitus inuadit, instinctu tam diuino sensus intimos et mobilitatem percipit, ut uel profanum intuentium uulgus in nouas ac prorsus improuisas prolectatum adfectiones cum corporum tum animorum motus propria perceptione sentire uideatur. en uiuida canis uis toto corpore contremiscentis, en quadrupes genibus submissis prolapsus in somnum siue iliis humi demissis in dorsum sese ex transuerso uolutans. hic indiscretae epheborum similitudines neruosa laterum intentione, dilatatis spiritu pulmonibus cursitant. nonnulla in publico, immo inter cottidianas populi consuetudines monumenta spectantur aptissime collocata. in Ecclesia Couentrensi pulpitum aquilinum patulo pinnarum fulcimento sacras scripturas sustinet. aedem suam sub diuo tutatur Sanctus Edmundus, rigida membrorum proceritate custos praegracilis. equitem offendunt Londinienses fumum et opes et strepitum exporrecta fronte despectantem, et qui iuxta Sancti Pauli deambulant pastorem mirantur pedo praetento quinque ouium gregem per plateam prosequentem. primas, puto, tenet matrona Sarisberiensis, quae capite erecto, corpore exili, obducta stola per pratulum firmo incedit gradu, nullum quidem infantis gestans onus, sed uultu seuero inenarrabile aerumnarum pondus arguens.

Praesento uobis Excellentissimi Ordinis Imperii Britannici Dominam Commendatricem, Collegii Newnhamensis honoris causa Sociam,

ELISABETHAM FRINK

F INALLY *we honour a sculptress in bronze. Her themes are taken from life and nature. Her unique gift is to penetrate so deeply beneath the outer surface of her subjects, so instinctively to apprehend their inmost feelings and the sense of their movement, that even the unpractised spectator is transported by a new and unexpected experience and instinctively senses and captures that movement and those feelings for himself. A dog, alert, trembles with life; horses lie sleeping, or roll over on the ground. Young men sprint, muscles tensed, lungs filled with air. Her statues find a natural home amid the everyday life of public places. Her Eagle Lectern spreads forth its wings in Coventry Cathedral. St Edmund, stiff-limbed and slender, keeps watch outside his cathedral at Bury. A horse and rider gaze calmly on the bustle of a London street, and a shepherd with crook outstretched directs his five sheep across the square beside St Paul's. Her masterpiece, a madonna, lean and erect, raiment gathered close about her, strides purposefully across the green at Salisbury, bearing no child in her arms, but on her countenance the burden of unfathomable care.*

I present to you

Dame ELISABETH FRINK,

Honorary Fellow of Newnham College.

41

HISPANIA, hinc montium Pyrenaeorum obice praemunita, illinc Oceani Atlantici et interni maris fluctibus interclusa, ut mercatores Poenici fingerent insulam et philologi commenticiae doctrinae obtentu Terram Reconditam intellegi uellent; stirpis alumna Celtiberae, cui mox Carthago Graecia colonos immiscuerunt; Romanarum flos prouinciarum, Principum mater Traiani Hadriani M. Aurelii Theodosii Magni; regnum Visigothorum ualidum, subinde Maurorum, post in plures disiuncta principatus, Legionem Castellam Aragoniam Nauarram, ipsis nominibus praeclara fabellarum gesta reboantes; aureae sub ortum aetatis in unum redintegrata, cum Ferdinandus Rex Isabella Regina coniunctis matrimonio potestatibus ultimum Maurorum regulum exterminarunt et aliena pro superstitione fidem confirmarunt Christianam; orbis dimidiae partis dominatrix, postquam Christophorus Columbus in occasum nauigauit et uictrices praedantium cateruae imperi transmarini fundamenta iecerunt; deinceps domesticis et exteris concussa cladibus pone marium et montium claustra denuo se recepit; donec sub Rege nominis Borboniensis herede decimo in unitatem libertatem prosperitatem uocata caput inter nationes Europaeas rursus extulit.

'Beatus qui ad regnum natus est' autumauit Franciscus de Quevedo 'modo in Regem regno dignum adolescat.' hospes hic noster, Rex regno dignissimus, hereditatem lubricis fortunae casibus obnoxiam uindicauit, uindicatam non sine periculo non sine gloria corroborauit: qui Romae natus exsul, tum cum patria calamitatibus omnium quas quaeuis uidit aetas maxime miserandis diuellitur, ad suos demum redux eruditionis tirocinium Matriti in Vniuersitate Complutensi, militiae apud classem legiones copias aerias emeritus anno aetatis septimo tricensimo tandem Rex pronuntiatur. liberis continuo suffragiis prouidet, legum nouarum promulgationi consulit, libertatis atque legum mox euadit summa re poscente uindex. quippe abhinc septuennio a.d. VII Kal. Mart. prima nocte praetoriani in curiam inrumpunt, uincula senatoribus, ruinam Reipublicae comminantes. Rex redeant in castra legionibus imperat, unum quemque legionis praefectum sacramento in nomen Reipublicae et Regis obligat, indutus paludamento coram populo uitam pro libertate deuouet. o singularem constantiam, o omni maiorem fide fortitudinem, o diem terque quaterque beatum, a quo 'omne aeui senium sua fama repellet', ut Lucani Cordubensis uerba mutuer. uidelicet illud quod uetustiore Hispanorum sollertia decantatum abierat in prouerbium 'iubent Reges, parent Leges' Rex rescidit refellit in contraria retorsit.

exinde perpetua aequanimitate et prudentia perspicaci ciuium uni-
uersorum gratiam atque adeo amorem, ciuitatium quot ubique sunt
liberarum conciliauit admirationem. idem hanc omnibus legem com-
mendauit atque sanxit, nullum regiminis uere popularis tutamen posse
firmius excogitari quam quod collocetur in auctoritate Regis. quid
enim? nonne omni ope atque opera enisus est ut partes regni dispares,
siue morum et linguae uarietate siue inueterata factionum aemulatione
distractas, in unum apte inter se cohaerentium membrorum quasi
corpus reducat? nonne Communitati Nationum Europaearum foedere
Romae icto Consociatarum nationem Hispanam consociatam reddidit?
nonne, qui tam fortiter pro libertate ciuitatis suae, pro ciuitatium
Europaearum unitate militauerit, praemio summo quod ab Imperatore
Carolo Magno nuncupatur rite donatus est?

Septem saeculorum annales si quis euoluet permulta nostrae cum
populo Hispano necessitudinis consanguinitatis familiaritatis depre-
hendet pignora: uelut Principum ille nostratium Ater cognominatus
Petrum Castellae suae regem reduxit, uelut Rex Alphonsus, eius
nominis tertius decimus, Principissam Victoriam Eugeniam augus-
tissimae Victoriae Reginae neptem in matrimonium duxit, uelut denique
hospes hic noster duos ante annos coram uno Procerum Populariumque
conuentu, quod nemini antehac concessum erat Regi exterorum,
contionatus est. iuuat ergo Academiam quoque Cantabrigiensem, quae
se sermonum institutorumque Hispanorum in cognitione non medio-
criter uersari gloriatur, erga Regem Hispanorum, erga populum
Hispanum suae ipsam pietatis uoluntatis gratulationis hoc qualecumque
pignus ostendere. uiuat Rex, uiuat Regina, uiuat Regia Domus, sitque
populo Hispano pax, sint euentus rerum cum Deo prosperi.

Praesento uobis

PRINCIPEM AVGVSTISSIMVM IOHANNEM CAROLVM HISPANIAE REGEM

SPAIN, *bounded by the Pyrenees and washed by two Oceans, so that Phoenician traders took her for an island and etymological fancy once explained her name as 'The Hidden Land'; inheritor of many races, Iberians from the South and Celts from the North, the Celtiberian stock enriched by Greek and Carthaginian colonists; most cultivated of the provinces of Rome, and mother of Emperors, Trajan, Hadrian, Marcus Aurelius, Theodosius the Great; mighty kingdom of the Visigoths, then caliphate of the Moors; once sundered into principalities whose names are resonant with romance, Leon, Castile, Aragon, Navarre; united at the dawning of a golden age, when Ferdinand and Isabella, joining their realms in marriage, expelled the last Muslim ruler from his palace in Granada and set up the cross of Christ in the mosques of the Alhambra; Queen of half the world, when Columbus sailed West and the Conquistadores founded an empire; in time, weakened by disasters domestic and foreign, retreating again behind the barriers of mountains and seas; she has, within our memory, emerged into a new era of unity, liberty, and prosperity, to raise her head high among the nations of Europe, under the leadership of her present King, the tenth monarch to inherit the royal title of the Spanish Bourbons.*

'Happy is the man who is born to be a King,' wrote Francisco de Quevedo, 'if, when he rules, he shows that he deserves to be one.' His Majesty's path to the throne and the establishment of his rule were paved with uncertainty and danger. Born in Rome, during an interregnum which witnessed the most tragic years of his country's history, he received a wide education in the Complutensian University of Madrid and in all three branches of the armed forces. Proclaimed King in his thirty-seventh year, he oversaw the first free elections in more than forty years and the promulgation of a new constitution. On the night of 23 February 1981, a date now stamped on the pages of history, when elements of the military burst into the Cortes, seizing the deputies and imperilling the democracy, single-handed he saved the State. Ordering the troops to return to barracks, he demanded of each army commander a personal commitment to the Crown and the Constitution. Wearing the full-dress uniform of Commander-in-Chief he was seen in almost every household in the land and vowed that he would lay down his life in defence of his country's freedom. Allá van leyes do quieren reyes (*'Where Kings wish, the Laws go'*) *says an old Spanish proverb.* Allá van reyes do quieren leyes (*'Where the Laws wish, Kings go'*) *was his message that day. By these actions of singular resolution and courage, 'whose fame' (in the words of the Roman*

poet Lucan, who was born at Cordoba) 'the lapse of years shall not decay',[1]
*and by the just and prudent statesmanship which have distinguished his
whole reign, he has established constitutional monarchy as the guardian
and guarantor of parliamentary democracy, and won the gratitude and
love of his own people and the admiration of all peoples of the free world.
He has further striven with exemplary dedication to draw together the
diverse parts of his kingdom, both regional and political, into a new unity,
to bring reconciliation where there was enmity, and harmony where there
was discord. And he has led his country into the Community of Nations
subscribing to the Treaty of Rome. For his services to the cause of
European co-operation and to the cause of democratic freedom he has been
honoured with the Charlemagne Prize.*

*The annals of seven centuries bear witness to the many ties of friendship
and blood which bind our two nations: from the days when the Black
Prince restored Peter I to the throne of Castile, to the marriage of His
Majesty's grandfather, King Alfonso XIII, with Princess Victoria Eugenia,
grand-daughter of Queen Victoria, and to the joyful occasion of His
Majesty's State Visit, two years ago, when he addressed both Houses of
Parliament, the first visiting monarch so to do. Today the University of
Cambridge, in which there flourishes the study of the cultures and
languages of the Spanish peoples, rejoices to offer His Majesty testimony
to its own affection and esteem both for his country and for himself. Long
live His Majesty; long live his Queen Consort; long live his Royal House;
and may his people be blessed, in God's grace, with prosperity and
peace.*

I present to you

HIS MAJESTY DON JUAN CARLOS I
KING OF SPAIN

[1] Lucan, 4. 812.

EST in Scholis Antiquis, alueario industriae feraci, Consilii Generalis cellula. ibi haec mulier, apium tamquam regina, unum et quadraginta dominabatur per annos, ita tamen ut nomine non suo sed Summi Consiliarii, non in exostra sed post siparium partes agere mallet. epistulas commentarios actorum breuiaria, quotquot fucorum examen introduxerat, aliud alii mandabat contubernalium, suum cuique pensum dispertiens, aut immani scriniorum tabulario consignabat, aut suae thesauro memoriae committebat, scriniis mehercule sescentis capaciori, in ordinem magis perfectum quam quoduis tabularium redacto. sciscitabantur Consiliarii quid potissimum rerum occasio postularet: rerum agendarum indices instruebat, instructos adnotatiunculis explicabat. si quid quando actum erat, acti testimonium dicto citius deprehendebat. si quas tabellas utpote in scriniis iamdudum absconditas longaeua obruerat obliuio, eas ne Molossica quidem canum uis fuisset odorandi sagacior. hanc omnes consulebant, consulentibus responsum dabat

> sanctius et multo certa ratione magis quam
> Pythia quae tripodi a Phoebi lauroque profatur.

hanc fidelitate nemo, nemo auctoritate superabat. crescit in dies negotiorum prouincia, crescit procurandi sollertia,

> inque dies crescens omnes stupor occupat, unum
> tot res ac tantas posse tenere caput.

tam cari capitis, cum ab alueo tandem discessit, quis desiderio modus? at semper honos huius et nomen et laudes manebunt, dum in cellulae uestibulo stat mnemosynon unicum, machinam dico computatricem, quae epistularum recenset introitus et exitus omnium. cui simul atque manum admoueris, extemplo FLORA TE SALVTAT.

Hodie pro tot ac tantis meritis par est ipsam ab Academia tota inuicem salutari

FLORAM EILEEN McLEOD CAREY

I N *that hive of industry, the Old Schools, is an inner cell, the Office of the General Board. And there, for forty-one years, a Queen Bee ruled. No ordinary Queen was she, for she gave herself no regal airs, and delegated executive authority to a Secretary General, and went by the name of his personal assistant. When the incoming mail arrived, or memoranda or minutes, she allotted them to the appropriate officer to deal with, or stored them away in their rightful places in her countless files, or committed them to her own capacious memory, which was less fallible and more orderly than any filing system. She prepared the agenda and drafted agenda notes for the meetings of the General Board and its innumerable Committees. When a precedent needed to be traced, she knew where to find it. When a document long consigned to the oblivion of a neglected file had to be recovered, her unerring instinct led her at once to the spot. When advice was called for, her answer came*

> *with reasoning more secure,*
> *Than once the Pythian priestess, wreathed in laurel,*
> *Descanted from the tripod of Apollo.*[1]

Her tact and discretion were absolute, the range and responsibility of her activities were without parallel and ever increased from day to day.

> *And still the wonder grew*
> *That one small head could carry all she knew.*[2]

And when the time came for her retirement, so sorely was she missed, so indispensable had her presence become, that a unique tribute was paid to her, by the creation of a computer program bearing her name, which records all letters which enter or leave the Office of the General Board. For when you switch on this program there flashes onto the screen the cheerful message WELCOME TO FLORA.

Today, in honouring a lifetime of devoted and selfless service, the whole University bids welcome to

FLORA EILEEN McLEOD CAREY

[1] Lucretius, 1. 738–9.
[2] Goldsmith, *The Deserted Village*, 215–16.

ROREM MARINVM, Mnemosynae sacrum, aptissimum sui insigne prae se fert illud quod hospita haec nostra fundauit magnum memoriae pietatisque monumentum. haec enim, dum malis praesentibus consulit, praeteritorum malorum memoriam non neglegit, et pietate eos potissimum complectitur qui uitas ultro profuderunt ut posteris uitae spem prorogarent. admodum adulescentula, auxiliariae medicarum pars una turmae, militum liberae Poloniae uindicum suprema discrimina sponte subeuntium spiritum agnouit ingenuum, excelsum, omnem laudem supergressum. bello exstincto uidit Europae ruinas, uidit sescentorum lacrimas, uidit a domo et patria extorres et omni subsidio ac spe carentes. carceres et nosocomia frequentat, artem medicinalem suppetit, nouum uitae destinatum ui uastatis suggerit. decedit demum curatio publica, priuatam decernit supponere. hospitium primum in Germania condit, quod adulescentibus sit receptaculum quos malesuada corrupit necessitas. e tali natus semine ros marinus increscit, florescit, radices latius semper extendit. aliud alii hospitium superadditur: exstant hoc temporis populos penes tredecim plus octoginta. et cui non notum hospitium illud in comitatu Suffolciae finibus nostris paene conterminum, ipsam ipsius dico domum, quod cum adoptiua tamquam familia sicut una materfamilias communicat, marito simul operam suam conferente, uiro pro hospitiis suo nomine conditis laude non impari praedicando? huius nempe mulieris acta reputanti subueniunt Sancti Ignatii uerba: nam mulierem descripsi quae nec periculo nec industriae nec impensae pepercit, quae praemium nullum, nullam requietem laborum poposcit.

Praesento uobis mulierem praehonorabilem, Praeclari Ordinis Sancti Michaelis et Sancti Georgii Sociam,

SVSANNAM Baronissam RYDER de VARSAVIA

'ROSEMARY – *that's for remembrance'*, said Ophelia. A sprig *of rosemary is the chosen emblem of the noble Foundation of our next honorand: a Foundation created for the relief of present suffering, as a living memorial to the sufferings of the past, lest we forget. As a nurse in the First Aid Nursing Yeomanry, attached to the Polish Section of Special Operations Executive, she was witness to the selfless cheerful courage of men and women embarking on missions of singular hazard. After the war she worked in the ruins of Europe, in hospitals and prisons, among the sick, destitute, and homeless. And when the official relief organisations folded their tents she began to pitch her own. She founded her first Home in Germany, a refuge for boys who had turned to crime in the desolation of the aftermath of war. And the sprig of rosemary grew, and its roots spread wide and deep, and Home followed upon Home, until today, in thirteen countries, more than eighty are found, in which the sick and disabled find new life and purpose, and not least in that Home which stands not far from here, her own family home at Cavendish in Suffolk, which, with her husband, himself the founder of Homes, she adapted to serve the needs of her extended family. To such a life we may aptly apply the words of the prayer of St Ignatius Loyola: for she has striven and has not counted the cost, she has fought and has not heeded the wounds, she has toiled and has not sought for rest, she has laboured and has not asked for any reward.*

I present to you the Right Honourable

SUE Baroness RYDER OF WARSAW, C.M.G.

EST in Collegii Sanctae et Indiuiduae Trinitatis sacello Isaaci Newtoni sigillum, cuius uiri

> uiuida uis animi peruicit et extra
> processit longe flammantia moenia mundi
> atque omne immensum peragrauit mente animoque.

en titulo cathedraeque successorem Newtonianae, immensos mundi ac temporis tractus impetu non impari permetientem. peregrinationis exordium a lacteis astrorum coetibus fecit, speciosa deprompturus inde miracula.

> nam fit uti exhausto genitali fomite sidus
> corruat interdum ac se in puncti contrahat instar,
> corpore condenso tamen et tanto grauitatis
> pondere adhuc pollens ut ne scintilla quidem una
> luminis inde queat molirier effugium ullum.
> quippe docet quae sint haec caeca foramina caeli,
> quos generent radios extremo in margine, qua ui
> hanc summam rerum uisam non uisa gubernent.
> tunc aliud pertemptat iter: descendit ab astris
> ut pauxillarum uisat uim particularum.
> nam quae corpora cumque immani maximitate
> praedita sunt, certis per foedera naturai
> ordinibus currunt et certis legibu' parent
> (sic certe graui' Newtoni sententia sanxit);
> at contra minimi res ponderi', corpora prima
> quas uocitare suëmus, ab omni lege solutae
> ordine non certo incassum uolitare uidentur.
> hic ergo, ne res permagnas perque minutas
> dissimili ratione geri fingamus inepte,
> omnem materiem rerum praepandere pergit,
> quo peperit pacto mundum natura creatrix,
> num siet exitium caeli terraeque futurum:
> scilicet infinitam aetatem temporis omnis
> uno suauidico ualuit contraxe libello.

Praesento uobis Excellentissimi Ordinis Imperii Britannici Commendatorem, Doctorem in Philosophia, Collegii Gonuillii et Caii Socium, Aulae Sanctae Trinitatis honoris causa Socium, Mathematices Professorem Lucasianum,

STEPHANVM GVLIELMVM HAWKING

IN the chapel of Trinity College stands the figure of Isaac Newton,

> The marble index of a mind forever
> Voyaging through strange seas of thought alone.[1]

Here is the present heir to Newton's title, embarked on a voyage of equal ambition, into the infinities of space and time. He first turned his thoughts to the galaxies, where a star in its death throes, its fuel exhausted, collapses to a point of matter infinitesimal in size, yet in mass so dense, in gravity so powerful, that not even light can escape. He has plumbed with mathematics the mysteries of these Black Holes, and discovered what radiation is generated at their surfaces, what power these invisible ghostly voids exert on the visible universe. From the vast spaces where stars live and die with predictability, he has travelled to the subatomic world, where elementary particles obey a contrary law, the law of uncertainty. To reconcile the laws which relate to phenomena on the largest scale, the gravitational laws of Newton and the relativity of Einstein, with the law which relates to the small, the uncertainty principle of quantum mechanics, and in so doing to devise a new and unified theory which will explain the nature and behaviour of all matter, how the universe came into being, and how it developed, and how it may end, is today the greatest intellectual challenge of theoretical science. And in the pursuit of this goal he is the standard-bearer and guide. Fired by a passion to communicate, he has encapsulated in one slim volume's best-selling pages, with a limpid style and engaging wit, a whole Brief History of Time.

I present to you

STEPHEN WILLIAM HAWKING, C.B.E., PH.D.,

Fellow of Gonville and Caius College, Honorary Fellow of Trinity Hall, Lucasian Professor of Mathematics.

---

[1] Wordsworth, *The Prelude*, 3. 62–3. The Latin speech quotes Lucretius, 1. 72–4.

DOCTORIS in Musica numquid palla pulchrius? quamquam quid incrementum pulchritudinis uel hoc purpurae decus tantae atque tali musices antistitae conferat, quae omnia quotquot ubique sunt theatra uocis claritate et formae maiestate decorauit? haec nempe, quae fabulas scaenicas, uernarum nenias, quae modos Henrici Purcell uetustos, Arnoldi Schoenberg nouicios, quae Mauriti Ravel Francogallas, Germanas Gustaui Mahler cantiunculas interpretetur, nullum cantandi genus non tetigit, nullum quod tetigit non adornauit.

> cor meum tandem tua uox recludit,
> ut rosae sese reserant, benigni
> cum sub aurora redeunte solis
> oscula libant.

primum de Berolinensibus egit triumphum, dum Elisabethae personam Wagnerianae sustinet. mox Cassandram cantauit Londini: ui uicti Troes, uoce uicti Londinenses. o caelestis Aida, quot mouisti Mediolanensibus suspiria! quantum tuis, Ariadna, Vindobonenses adflerunt fletibus! quae, cum hanc contuemur, heroinarum pompa procedit! nonne amore percussas graui Sieglindam Elissam Penelopen Alcestin, nonne flamma leuiore combustas Helenam nec non Amadei Comitissam cernere uidemur? nonne, cum Didonem producit postrema lugentem, cum Bruennhildam uel Isoldam extrema meditantes, cum quattuor Ricardi Strauss cantus supremos, pectus tangit nescioquid supra mortalitatem?

> sic est, uocamur: iam uideo deam:
> complexa pinnis me leuat aureis
> curaque mortali remotum
> adserit in numerum deorum.

Praesento uobis Collegii Newnhamensis et Collegii Iesu honoris causa Sociam

JESSYE NORMAN

WE reserve our most beautiful robe until last. And yet what increment of beauty can even such a robe bestow on this high priestess of song, who has illumined stages and concert halls the world over with her lustrous voice and majesty of person? From Purcell to Schönberg, from the Lieder of Mahler to the chansons of Ravel, from grandest opera to the negro spirituals of her native Georgia, no musical genre has she not essayed, none has she essayed but she has adorned.

> Mon coeur s'ouvre à ta voix,
> Comme s'ouvrent les fleurs
> Aux baisers de l'aurore.[1]

Berlin was the scene of her earliest triumph, as Wagner's Elisabeth. She sang Cassandra in The Trojans, and Covent Garden, no less than Troy, was taken by storm. A celestial Aida enraptured La Scala, Vienna wept for her love-lorn Ariadne. Oh what a pageant of heroines passes before us! All the sorrows of Elsa, Sieglinde, Alceste, Pénélope, and the lighter passions of la belle Hélène and Mozart's Contessa. And when we hear her sing the last lament of Dido, or the dying testaments of Brünnhilde and Isolde, or the Four Last Songs of Richard Strauss, do we not seem to approach one step nearer to heaven?

> Ja, es stieg auch mir ein Engel nieder,
> Und auf leuchtendem Gefieder
> Führt er, ferne jedem Schmerz,
> Meinen Geist nun himmelwärts.[2]

I present to you

JESSYE NORMAN,

Honorary Fellow of Newnham and Jesus Colleges.

---

[1] 'My heart opens at your voice, as the flowers open at the kisses of the dawn' (Saint-Saëns, Samson et Dalila). 'When I was about twelve years old, one of my first big arias was Mon coeur s'ouvre à ta voix', Miss Norman once said in an interview.

[2] 'Yes, an angel has come to me, and with shining golden wings carries my spirit, far from every pain, upwards to heaven' (Wagner, Wesendonck Lieder, a work which Miss Norman has performed at the Last Night of The Proms).

O DIEM laetum et calculo notandum candido, cum theatrum sumptibus suis fundatum inter celeberrimam musicorum et saltatorum festiuitatem Maynardus ille Keynes his uerbis dedicauit: 'Ne ab hac Vrbe exsulent Artes, en uobis theatrum, urbani academicique Cantabrigienses, fiduciariis concredo, en uobis aedem, Euterpe, Erato, Melpomene, Terpsichore, et recens deabus addita Cinesithea, noua Pieridum pentas, pentagoniam consecro.' sic ab auspicio bono profectum surgit prouincialium decus theatrorum, hospes magni iam nominis histrionum, nutrix in magnum postera laude crescentium.

Genium theatri uidetis adstantem. priores autem in re nauali partes gerebat: primum in naue uectoria dispensator creatus stipendia meruit, mox tormentis bellicis in mari Cretico uerberatus est, restituta pace Nortuegiae Melitae postremo domi summis uiris res maritimas administrantibus a manu praesto fuit. quid mirum si e fluctibus euasit imperator histricus? nam quis homine salso insulsas histrionum procellas paratior perpeti? dicterium certe illud Shauianum

> si quem deus uult perdere, dementat prius,
> postid magistrum scaenici gregis facit

explosit exturbauit exsibilauit. quippe praedicamus uirum supra modum prudentem, rei nummariae sollertem, ingenio multiplici et ad omnia uersatili praeditum. adcedere animum ad amicitiam promptum ex eo colligas quod uoluntatem atque adeo amorem sicut nemo conciliauit cum omnium quotquot ubique sunt scaenicorum tum nostratium qui nunc sunt quique olim fuerunt tirunculorum. testes adduco Marlouianos, Lucipedorum ludiones, cantatores cothurnatos siue soccatos, fabulas Atticas quarto quoque anno renatas, alterum denique illud theatrum Rosculis AcaDemiCis destinatum. quibus hic omnibus firma manu, consiliis salutaribus, incredibili quadam facultate simul uirtutes fouendi, simul imprudentias coercendi nimium quantum profuit.

Praesento uobis uirum et Vrbi et Academiae commendatum, Excellentissimo Ordini Imperii Britannici adscriptum,

ANDREAM RONALDVM BLACKWOOD

FIFTY *years and more ago, Lord Keynes built a theatre at his own expense and presented it in trust to the University and the City. Heaven smiled on the theatre in its infancy. A Gala Performance was announced. The Sadlers Wells orchestra played, Constant Lambert conducted, Margot Fonteyn and Frederick Ashton danced. The programme proudly proclaimed the founder's aim: 'The object of the Arts Theatre of Cambridge is the entertainment of the University and Town. Its name describes, and the form of a pentagon given to its auditorium by the architect symbolises, its purpose of providing a home in Cambridge for the five arts of drama, opera, ballet, music and cinema'. It has risen to be the glory of provincial theatres, host to the greatest in the land, and nurse of young talent which has gone forth to greatness.*

Foremost among those to whom credit is due is the man now before you, for thirty-two years presiding genius of the Arts. He came to the theatre from the sea. He had served as a purser with the Olsen Line; while on active service in the war, he was bombarded in Crete and torpedoed in the Mediterranean; he became Assistant Naval Attaché in Norway, where he received the King Haakon Cross, then Secretary to Admiral Mountbatten in Malta; and he finally served as acting Commander in the Ministry of Defence. All this was good training for his second career. It gave him a salty sense of humour, with which he has weathered many a histrionic storm. 'No man becomes a theatre manager,' quipped Shaw, 'unless the gods have destroyed his reason.' In this man, they erred: for they gave him an uncommon measure of common sense, financial acumen of the highest order, a readiness to learn and adapt, and above all a genius for friendship, which have won him the admiration and affection of the theatrical world at large and of generations of our own undergraduates. The Marlowe Society, the Footlights, the Opera Society, the Gilbert and Sullivan Society, the triennial Greek Play, our own University theatre the ADC – all these, far beyond the call of duty, he has guided with a steady hand and encouraged with wise advice, bringing out their best and preserving them from the worst of their follies.

I present to you a man who has earned the applause of Town and Gown alike,

ANDREW RONALD BLACKWOOD, M.B.E.,

lately General Manager of the Arts Theatre and Secretary of the Arts Theatre Trust.

'OMNIVM rerum mensura est homo' dixit Protagoras. at enim res nonnullae tantulis procedunt motibus ut uix aetas Tithoni, nedum hoc aeui quodcumque est, earum processum metiendi sit capax, aliae tam caeco uel pernici cursu mouentur ut non Argi caput centum luminibus cinctum prosequi possit. quo, quaeso, deprehendas experimento solum uix ac ne uix quidem de colle derepens uel immensam niuis congelatae molem uallibus defluentem? uel si lapillos demergas mari, quae mane, quae mense postero, quae mille post annis mensura migrationis?

Harum rerum mensorem adduco nulli secundum, qui amplius decem lustra geographorum nostratium inuestigationibus cum summam in re fabrili sollertiam tum natiuum inuentionis instinctum impertiebat. si quis quando instrumenti cuiuspiam rudem atque indigestam notionem mente conceperat, hic instrumentum ad amussim perfectum pariebat e materia saepius extemporali. tum quot in officinae confiniis praestigias exhibebat! quas pluuias excitabat, quos amnium maeandros elaborabat! quot uentis quot harenas congerebat, quot litora quot fluctibus uerberabat! glaciem fingit, fictam fictae conualli superponit: en germanum glaciei defluuium, en crepaturas ueris ueriores! ipsam naturam nempe simulabat, immo superabat ingenio suo, nam citius quam natura, di magni, rem peregit. an de lapillorum aenigmate solutio poscitur? lapillos terebrauit, quos radiis loquacibus refertos, quamuis aestui mobili obnoxios, auritae machinationes aucuparentur. adcedit et hoc, quod explorationum longius deductarum prodibat non semel particeps, simul fidus doctis contubernalibus Achates, simul suorum ipsius instrumentorum periclitabundus, non aegre, puto, desideratae redux officinae, quippe ubi inuentis bos nullus insultaret, ouis nulla se ingurgitaret.

Praesento uobis artificem uere regium

ALFREDVM HENRICVM KING

'**M**AN *is the measure of all things', said Protagoras. But some things move so slowly that a hundred lifetimes would not suffice for man to measure their movement; others move so fast or so inconstantly that not even the mythical Argus with his hundred eyes could keep track of them. What is the rate and form of a glacier's flow? How fast does soil creep down a hillside? If you place a pebble on the sea bed, where will it be next morning? Where in a month's time? Where in a millennium?*

For more than half a century one man has placed his consummate craftsmanship and instinctive flair for improvisation at the service of our geographers in their attempts to answer such questions as these. They brought him ideas and designs for novel laboratory, field and teaching equipment. The equipment emerged, often from the most rudimentary materials, perfectly made and ideally suited to the job. His art in the laboratory helped rain to fall there, rivers to flow and meanders to form, the wind to blow and sand dunes to heap up, waves to break and beaches to develop, clay glaciers to move and crevasses to open. Such imitation of nature on a smaller scale enables us to see in a few hours what nature itself took millions of years to achieve; and observations and measurements made in this microcosm assist in the understanding of the same phenomena in the real world. But to return to the pebbles on the sea bed – he drilled holes in the pebbles, which were then filled with radioactive material and dropped in the sea off the coast, so that a Geiger counter could chart their changing locations. Into the field, too, he has ventured himself, to give first hand assistance with scientific observations and to test and refine his equipment. I suspect that he always returned with relief to his laboratory, for there, at least, there were no cows to trample or sheep to nibble his inventions.

I present to you a master craftsman, a king, not in name alone, among technicians,

ALFRED HARRY KING,

formerly of the Department of Geography.

IOHANNEM Christianum Smuts, sanctae uirum memoriae, Can-cellariatus nostri quondam decus, huic praeconio praefigere par et decorum est. adest enim quae huius in uerba iurauit, Vnitarum ductoris Partium, cum primum relictis Academiae umbraculis ad fori descendit puluerem. mox Partibus disiectis nec iam uero nomine Vnitis, ut quae repulsas in comitiis et ductoris mortem tulissent, in nouas Progredientium digressa Partes undecim cum sociis senator creata est, postmodo sola sociorum superstes futura. neque ipsos tantum quorum est electa suffragiis sed uniuersam hominum suffragio carentium nationem in clientelam suam uindicauit. exinde in muti senatus obsequio, compressis exilio aut carcere Afrorum primoribus, cum Princeps Ministrorum gentium seiunctionem decerneret, Minister Iustitiae rem publicam legibus oppressam nomine salutis contineret, haec una uocem rumpebat aduersariam, tredecim per annos immane sustinens onus, una suae factionis interpres, una legum quarumlibet censor, una quibusuis de rebus orator. o Helenam rediuiuam, quae si non mille deduxit carinas nec ui uicit Pergami turres, mille tamen quaestiones, mille contiones in magistratus librauit et infandae dominationis arcem tormentis uerberauit. quae nil probra, nil fastus morata, uel amara lento temperans risu, tam molesta quam occinens in spineto cicada (ut maledictum uertamus in laudem), spem libertatis exstingui non sinebat, si quando forte dies optatus ille, cuius aduentum iam iam prouidemus, nullis non gentibus aequum lumen tolleret.

Praesento uobis Excellentissimi Ordinis Imperii Britannici honoris causa Dominam Commendatricem, Reipublicae Africae Australis olim Senatorem, Aulae Nouae honoris causa Sociam,

HELENAM SUZMAN

THE *name of Jan Christiaan Smuts is honoured among the nations; it is honoured in this University, of which he was Chancellor; it is honoured not least in the heart of our next honorand. A lecturer in economic history in the University of the Witwatersrand, she entered political life in the last year of his Premiership, as a member of the United Party, of which he was leader. But the Party was soon ousted from office by electoral defeat, and soon deprived of its leader by death, and, when she entered Parliament, it was united no longer. A group of twelve seceded, among which she was one, to form a new Progressive Party, of which she was shortly to remain as the solitary representative in Parliament. Elected by the votes of her ten thousand constituents, she took as her true constituency the whole voteless black population of twenty millions. With the official opposition mute, and the black political leaders in exile or in prison, she was the sole voice of authentic Parliamentary opposition, as the Prime Minister of those days issued his apartheid legislation and the Minister of Justice constructed a police state of security laws. To become her Party's spokeswoman on every sector of national affairs, to analyse every Bill, to engage in every major debate: this was the mighty task which she shouldered alone for thirteen long years. A Helen who launched not a thousand ships but a thousand questions and speeches at the governing Party, who sacked no topless towers but struck with innumerable blows the bastions of inhumanity; untouched by obloquy and scorn, or repaying them with wit and repartee; as troublesome as the cricket in the thorn tree (we may turn to her credit what was said in dispraise);[1] she fanned the flickering flame of liberty, against that long awaited dawn, whose earliest rays we now behold, when the sun might shine with equal light on all the peoples of her land.*

I present to you

HELEN SUZMAN, HON. D.B.E.,

formerly Member of the House of Assembly, Parliament of the Republic of South Africa, and Honorary Fellow of New Hall.

---

[1] 'When she gets up in this House,' said a political opponent, 'she reminds me of a cricket in a thorn tree when it is very hot in the bushveld. His chirping makes you deaf, but the tune remains the same year in and year out.' *A Cricket in the Thorn Tree* is the title of the biography of Mrs Suzman by Joanna Strangwayes-Booth (1976).

ERAT unus Argonautarum Lynceus

> posset qui rumpere terras
> et Styga transmisso tacitam deprendere uisu.

Lynceo quid nunc opus? oculis oculatiores fiunt machinae, Styx linquenda theologis.

> innumerabilium iacularier electrorum
> uim uolucrem ualuit traiectu praepete per rem
> dumtaxat tenuem doctorum prisca potestas,
> ut rei traiectae mox transpiceretur imago
> quantumuis paruae quantumuis magnificata.
> in pugnam descendit homo, quem uiuida uirtus
> flagrat mente noua, non tenuia texta domandi
> sed condensarum pollentia pondera rerum.
> propterea studet electris sic imperitare
> ut corpus summum transuerso tramite lustrent,
> quodque superficiem nequeant transire, repulsu
> adsiduo reiecta ruant collectaque rursus
> perfectum summi dent corporis exemplare.

o perplexae rationis inuentionem. uix mirum si doctores exteri iam tantum temptauerant opus, temptatum spe depulsi reliquerant. hic nouae spei capax, quippe qui radiis speculatoriis per aera traiectis belli adiumenta fabricasset, tironum copias laborum consocias conuocauit, tirocinii magnum utique emolumentum prouidens, uel si spe fallerentur. nec spem fefellit euentus. tandem commilitones reducit praedae compotes, microscopii omnem supergressi fidem, imaginum feracis uero ueriorum, quasi rei superficiem simul a fronte, simul ex obliquo conspiceris. proba merx, quod aiunt, facile emptorem reperit. in tam probam microscopii mercem quis medicorum, quis biologorum, quis moles metallorum uel microelectricas minutias inquirentium non magno appetitu cucurrit?

Vir alienae uirtutis excultor adhuc similem se sui praestat. nempe in horto nunc otiatur, quo nullus potest uideri praestantior, flores suos sicut olim tirones in maius uirtutis prouehens.

Praesento uobis Equitem Auratum, Excellentissimo Ordini Imperii Britannici adscriptum, Magistrum in Artibus, Societatis Regiae Sodalem, Ingeniariae Electricae Professorem Emeritum, Collegii Sanctae et Indiuiduae Trinitatis Socium,

CAROLVM GVLIELMVM OATLEY

T HERE *was an Argonaut called Lynceus, so lynx-eyed that he could*

> *Transmit his piercing vision through the earth*
> *And open up the mysteries of Hell.*[1]

The range of the human eye, and even of the optical microscope, has been far outdistanced by electron optics. And for visions of Hell we now consult other authorities. First came the Transmission Electron Microscope, which catapulted a finely focused beam of electrons at enormous speed straight through a specimen. There was one drawback: the specimen must be very thin, permeable to electrons. Along came our honorand, with a bold new plan: to range the beam of electrons over the surface of the specimen in zig-zag fashion, like the pinpoint of light which races back and forth on our television screens, and to catch the electrons as they leapt away from the specimen, which could be as solid and impermeable as you like. Scientists abroad had tried this before, but they had failed, for the technical problems were of breathtaking complexity. Perhaps it was his work in radar during the war that prompted him to resume the endeavour. He guided a succession of remarkable graduate students, knowing that, even if the goal should elude them, there could be no better training for them than work of this kind. Together they solved the problems, one by one, and painstakingly realised and perfected his plan. And so the Scanning Electron Microscope was born, giving forth pictures with a depth of focus which passes belief, pictures which offer an image of three-dimensional reality in the microworld. It became a best seller, and today no laboratory is without one, for it is an essential tool in all scientific research, from metallurgy to medicine, from biology to microelectronics.

A scientist who, seeking no personal fame or glory, cultivated and brought forth the best in others, now in his retirement cultivates his marvellous garden in Porson Road, where the plants and flowers, like his students of old, respond to his guidance and give forth their best.

I present to you

Sir CHARLES WILLIAM OATLEY, O.B.E., M.A., F.R.S.,

Emeritus Professor of Electrical Engineering, Fellow of Trinity College.

---

[1] Valerius Flaccus, *Argonautica*, 1. 463–4.

VIS consili expers mole ruit sua,
uim temperatam di quoque prouehunt
in maius.[1]

In hospitem hunc nostrum si quem alium uerba Flacci cadunt, qui, dum multo consilio uires cum suas tum aliorum temperat, siue commeatus electricos administrando siue conturbatis consortionum maximarum rationibus prouidendo, magna ad fastigia rerum prouectus est. hic anno aetatis quinto decimo dimissis ludi magistris officinam Sodalitatis Electricae Birminghamensem ingressus horas subsiciuas institutioni suae dedidit, primum machinali, postea oeconomicae, ut accepti atque expensi custodes ipse custodiret. mox Caledoniae meridianae, post Angliae Cambriaeque toti uirium electricarum curationi praefectus est. 'uires' ut ait Vergilius 'adquirit eundo.'[2] consortioni Weir nominatae, postquam hic consilium adtulit, 'collectum robur *uire*sque refectae'. 'etiam sua Turn(er)um fata uocant': confestim 'Turn(er)i de uita et sanguine certat'. tertia deinde consortio, magni iam nominis umbra, postquam ex administratione publica in suam dicionem ab hoc est redacta, denuo probata machinarum suarum propulsione confisa suRRexit. 'extemplo magnas it fama per urbes': non mirum si Arcessitis Consiliariis Ob Scientiam Technologiamque praeponitur. o incredibilem munerum multitudinem. quae omnia cum laudare uix possim, nolim tamen silere Concilii Machinatorum Praesulem, Societatis Machinalis Socium et Propraesidem, Instituti Technologiae Cranfeldiensis Procancellarium, non in Scientiis tantum sed in Legibus etiam Litterisque Doctorem. si enim, quod Graeci dictitabant, ἀρχή ἄνδρα δείκνυσιν, noscite omnis Mineruae uirum, in officinarum puluere, in Academiarum umbraculis, in omni denique ciuitatis parte scientiarum promouendarum strenuum uindicem.

Praesento uobis uirum admodum honorabilem

FRANCISCVM LEONARDVM Baronem TOMBS de BRAILES

[1] Horace, *Odes*, 3. 4. 65–7.
[2] Vergil, *Aeneid*, 4. 175. For the following quotations see *Georgics*, 3. 235, *Aeneid*, 10. 471–2, 12. 765, 4. 173.

'POWER, *without good management, collapses under its own weight*' said Horace. '*Power, well managed, the gods advance to new heights.*' *Was the poet thinking of the electricity supply industry, of which our honorand was for many years the cornerstone? Or the industrial companies which he has rescued from the brink of bankruptcy? At all events, here is a man who, by insisting on good management in others, and by displaying an abundance of good management himself, has become a power in the land. He left school at the age of fifteen to join the General Electric Company, and trained as an engineer by taking evening classes at the Birmingham College of Technology. He later found time to gain an external degree in Economics at London, in order, he said, to keep an eye on accountants. He managed the South of Scotland Electricity Board, and became Chairman of the Electricity Council for England and Wales. By now his batteries were fully charged, and he was called in to give a new boost to the failing fortunes first of the Weir Group, then of Turner and Newall. It was hardly surprising that Rolls-Royce (for the name of the Rolls is still synonymous with the best that British engineering can offer) should invite him to guide it back into the private sector, in which it now soars aloft on new wings, or rather on its traditional aero-engines. His fame reached Whitehall, and he was summoned by the Prime Minister to be Chairman of the Advisory Council on Science and Technology. 'Office' says the Greek proverb 'reveals the man.' The offices which he has held, and the honours which he holds (so numerous that I add only, by way of illustration, that he is a past Chairman of the Engineering Council, a Fellow and past Vice-President of the Fellowship of Engineering, Pro-Chancellor of the Cranfield Institute of Technology, and holds honorary Doctorates not only in Science but also in Law and Letters) reveal a man of many parts held together by a unifying thread, a deep commitment to the promotion of scientific development, research, and education in every sphere of national life.*

I present to you The Right Honourable

FRANCIS LEONARD Baron TOMBS OF BRAILES

EN historiae mediaeualis antistitem, Aquarum diu Sextiarum, nunc Lutetiae decus, Academiae Francogallicae coetui caelesti recens additum deum. hic olim compilatis abbatiae Cluniacensis tabulariis regionem Matisconensem descripsit magnis concussam motibus et in nouum feodalis quae uocatur societatis ordinem corruentem. o indolis rarae dissertationem, quae multos sui in aemulationem traxit, nemini laudes concessit primarias. postea libris ceu de perenni fonte diuulgatis totam Europam occidentalem prospectu latiore complexus talium motuum naturam causas euentus scrutatus est, non uitae tantum et cultus hominum sed etiam mentium et sensuum curiosus. nam aedis euanidae lineamenta, picti parietis gypsum putrescens, familiarum stemmata, Pontificales epistulas, quodcumque quantulumcumque non obruit longaeuae uetustatis obliuio, e muto monumento uiuidum uitae testem facit. uidelicet 'in altis Museorum silentiis auscultando, chartulas puluerulentas interrogando, si quid clanculum mussitent, uitam humanam, qualis fuerit, aucupari decet'. o somniorum somnio illo Scipionis magis diuinorum somniatorem, o manium e sepulcris in luminis oras euocatorem. nonne huc equitantem uidemus Gulielmum Marescallum, nonne hos proelium Bouinense redintegrantes? ecce nos ipsos sacerdotes milites pauperes, en glebas ligonibus uersamus, ecclesias cathedrales elaboramus, anni millensimi aduentum contremiscimus. o eximium uerborum artificem, nec modo lectoribus sed uel ipsis inTVentibus commendatum. an numquam otiatur? immo e macellis et angiportibus Parisinis, si quando licet, in Prouinciam suam se abripit, ut ambulationibus longinquis inter oleas ac pineta recreetur.

Praesento uobis Societatum Mediaeualium in Collegio Francogallico Professorem, Academiae Britannicae hospitis iure Socium,

GEORGIVM MICHAELEM CLAVDIVM DUBY

HERE is a prince among medievalists, long lauded in Aix-en-Provence, now lauded in Paris, and lately installed in the pantheon of the immortels, as a Member of the Académie Française. In his earliest book he illustrated, largely from the archives of the Benedictine abbey of Cluny, the momentous change from the old order to that social structure known to us as feudal society, as it was seen in the region of Mâcon in the eleventh and twelfth centuries. It was a pioneering work, which has inspired many regional studies, and remains unsurpassed among them. Thereafter, in books issued in an unending stream, he has enlarged the field of his vision to embrace the whole of western Europe during the early Middle Ages. He is a historian of society, but no less a historian of ideas, a master of material fact, but no less of ideologies, collective attitudes, mentalités. Each relic of the past, the ground-plan of an abbey long vanished, the crumbling plaster of a painted wall, genealogical histories, papal letters, material mute and inert, he has transformed into witnesses with life and voice. 'We must always be looking' (he says) 'beneath the dust of our documents and listening in the silence of museums for man as he really was'. He is a dreamer, a sorcerer: from crypts and graveyards he calls forth the dead to live again, and turns back the centuries, so that present and past are one. We ride by the side of Guillaume le Maréchal, we battle at Bouvines, we are peasants and warriors and priests, we till the land and build the cathedrals, we tremble at the approach of the millennium. 'Le style est l'homme même', said Buffon. And what style he has! Not only on the page, but on television too – for the médiéviste is a consummate médiatiste. Does he ever rest? Yes, his greatest delight is to leave his appartement in Les Halles and seek inspiration in long walks among the pines and olives of his beloved Provence.

I present to you

GEORGES MICHEL CLAUDE DUBY,

Holder of the Chaire d'Histoire des Sociétés Médiévales in the Collège de France, Corresponding Fellow of the British Academy.

ΠΟΛΛΑ τὰ δεινά, scripsit Sophocles. quidni addidisset κοὐδὲν loliginis δεινότερον πέλει? haec enim atramenti expulsione praedantibus os sublinit, aquarum siphonibus prorsus emissis sua se in uestigia receptat, et quo pernicior sensuum e neruis in musculos fiat commeatus fibra se instruxit omnium maxima, axone qui dicitur giganteo, materie hospitis nostri experimentis adprime accommodata. nempe axon iste, sicut noster deprehendit, stimulo quouis excitatus in foedus uirium electricarum contrarium confestim traducitur, in confirmatiuum scilicet pro negatiuo. res mira, causa traductionis aegre explicanda. explicationem ingeniosissimam excogitauit, excogitatam experimentis subtilibus comprobauit. uidelicet simulatque neruum excitauisti reclusis quae in membrana locantur canalibus modo intromittuntur ἰόντα natrii, confirmatiuae capacia potestatis, sensuum per fibram internuntia, post extruduntur ἰόντα potassii, donec uiribus electricis in foedus pristinum restitutis neruus denuo conquiescat. tam praeclara propter reperta non mirum si una cum Andrea suo Huxley, operis consorte, nobelitatus est. num laureis arreptis otiatur? immo nouam animalium consortionem aduocat, quorum potentiam inuestiget oculatam.

> Limule procedas, Amblystoma curre Tigrinum;
> tu quoque cum Chelydra, Bufo Marine, ueni.

his operum fisus consortibus alteram inuestigationis uiam ingressus est euentu non minus prospero. nempe qua uirium electricarum quae oculi cellulis insunt immutatione fiat ut lux pupillae incidens imagines extrinsecus natas cum cerebro communicet certa perspectum ratione patefecit.

Praesento uobis electrophysiologorum Nestora, Equitem Auratum, Ordini insigniter Meritorum adscriptum, Doctorem in Scientiis, Collegii Sanctae et Indiuiduae Trinitatis Socium et olim Magistrum, Biophysices Professorem Emeritum, Collegii Girtonensis honoris causa Socium, Societatis Regiae Socium et olim Praesidem,

ALANVM LLOYD HODGKIN

'THE WORLD *has many marvels, but none more marvellous*' (*Sophocles might have said*) '*than the squid*'. *It can baffle pursuit with a cloud of ink, or move swiftly backwards by jet-propulsion. And it has developed the largest of all nerve fibres, the giant axon, for rapid transmission of the nerve impulses which activate its muscles. Our honorand was not slow to realise what perfect experimental material was provided by an axon so conveniently large. He measured the electrical potential inside the axon, and found that this potential was reversed, from negative to positive, as soon as the nerve was excited. He hypothesised, and proved his hypothesis by a series of complex experiments and even more complex mathematics, that the excitation of the nerve opens channels in the surrounding membrane, through which positively charged sodium ions flow inwards, generating the impulse which is conducted along the nerve fibre, until the opening of further channels allows the outflow of potassium ions, which restores the potential difference across the membrane and returns the nerve to its inactive state. This work, performed in partnership with his Trinity colleague Andrew Huxley, was crowned with the highest award which science can bestow. But he was not content to rest on his Nobel laurels. Now he focussed his attention on the eye, and with a novel phalanx of aquatic life to help him, the horseshoe crab, the snapping turtle, the tropical toad, and the salamander, he embarked on a further series of triumphantly successful experiments, in which he showed how light, by altering the electrical current in the retina's photoreceptor cells, is converted into a signal conveying information to the brain.*

I present to you a man who has transformed our understanding of the nervous system,

Sir ALAN LLOYD HODGKIN, o.m., sc.d.,

Fellow and formerly Master of Trinity College, Emeritus John Humphrey Plummer Professor of Biophysics, Honorary Fellow of Girton College, Fellow and past President of the Royal Society.

S CVRRAM quis nescit Bellocianum?

> libenter, ut uir optumas,
> audit ruinas uitreas.

quem quantum antecellit hospes hic noster, qui tot uitri se pondera perfregisse fateatur, quot ne Archytas quidem, numero carentis harenae mensor, enumeret. quippe quondam, si notae quam optimae uitrum postulabatur, nonnisi lima terendo, limatum poliendo, sudore multo, sumptu maximo, intertrimento uitri non pusillo constabat euentus. ergo liquefactum uitrum liquefacto cassitero iussit superfundi, ut unus perpetuus uitreus amnis simul prolaberetur, simul refrigesceret, donec solido concretus corpore posset incolumis abstrahi. en uitrum omni labe liberum, omni lima limatius, cui palmam splendoris fons Bandusiae deferat. in tantum inuentionis miraculum omnes qui ubique sunt uitrarii confestim cucurrerunt. o Archimeden alterum, immo alterum Icarum, ponto uitreo nomina daturum.

Idem penes nos tergeminis honoribus ob tergeminam pila ludendi sollertiam fulsit. nec Academiae suae umbraculorum oblitus est, dum officinarum se inmiscet pulueri. numquid, rogat, officinatores et academici contrariis inter se negotiis distrahuntur? quidni firmiore necessitudinis uinculo copulentur? hercle tam hos quam illos saluti suae scitius esse prouisuros, si scientiae studentibus potius quam accepti atque expensi computatoribus rem summam concredant administrandam. tam egregie cordatum uirum quid mirum si Fundatio Cantabrigiensis, nobis in posterum spes ac salus, Praesulem nuper adsciuit?

Praesento uobis Equitem Auratum, Magistrum in Artibus, Regiae Societatis Sodalem, Collegii Sanctae et Indiuiduae Trinitatis honoris causa Socium, Consortionis Pilkingtonianae Praesidem,

LIONELEM ALEXANDRVM BETHVNE
(siue ALASTARVM) PILKINGTON

D o you remember the exploits of John Vavassour de Quentin Jones?

> Like many of the upper class
> He liked the sound of broken glass.[1]

But Belloc's hero is no match for our next honorand, who, in perfecting his new method of glass manufacture, admits to breaking 100,000 tons of it. Not long ago, if you wanted plate glass of high quality, you had to get it by grinding and polishing, with much expenditure of energy and money and much wastage of glass. His inspired idea for eliminating the grind and the polish was to pass a continuous ribbon of molten glass direct from the furnace on to a bath of molten tin and float it down the bath, through a gradually reducing temperature, until the glass was sufficiently cool and hard to be taken off the liquid. And it worked: the glass emerged, its surfaces perfectly flat and parallel, without distortion or imperfection, with a polish that neither man nor machine could give. By this technique, a bold and brilliant break with tradition, he has revolutionised the manufacture of glass worldwide – a modern Archimedes, nay a modern Icarus, that other high-flier who (as Horace puts it) 'gave his name to a glassy sea'.[2]

At Cambridge he won Blues for tennis, squash, and fives. And the interests of the Universities have always remained close to his heart. He holds a passionate conviction that Industry and the Universities need each other, and that both would work better if run by the engineer and not by the accountant. When a man has views as sound and enlightened as these, it is not surprising that we should invite him to lead our campaign to attract outside support for our long-term needs, as first ever Chairman of the Cambridge Foundation.

I present to you

Sir LIONEL ALEXANDER BETHUNE (ALASTAIR) PILKINGTON, M.A., F.R.S.,

President, Pilkington plc, Honorary Fellow of Trinity College.

---

[1] Belloc, New Cautionary Tales.
[2] Horace, Odes, 4. 2. 3–4.

NON me religio, non lex, non ulla uoluntas
mascula militiam cogit inire meam.

Vox Yeatsiana quam apte in hanc mulierem cadit, nouae uoluntatis
interpretem, noui rerum ordinis nuntiam, inueteratarum uictricem
factionum. quae postquam institutioni iudiciali in Collegio Dublinensi
Sanctae Trinitatis et in Schola Legum Haruardiana se dedidit, ad
Dublinenses suos redux adhuc unguis teneri puella cum Iuris Professor
tum in superiore curiae consessu Senator creata est. fit uxor, fit trium
mater liberorum, artibus professoriis addit usum fori. pro feminis, pro
ciuibus aequo iure destitutis, pro omni humanitatis et liberalitatis causa
militat. mecastor huc usque audentiae peruenit ut domestica reipublicae
instituta ad iurisdictionis Europaeae puluerem prouocet. Laborantium
confirmata suffragiis bis consessum inferiorem petit, bis in comitiis fert
repulsas. ad maiorem se adcingit gloriam et summum suo tempore
adfectat magistratum, priuata mulier, nullis obstricta partibus, omnium
consensu uoti prorsus exspes. nullam non urbem, nullam non insulam
uisitat, circum pagos et compita uolat. palmam adepta sic conciuibus
contionatur: 'uobis, uiri mulieresque Hibernici, acceptam refero
nostram uictoriam, qui uestris sententiis, uestra uirtute confisi, non
partibus sed reipublicae consulentes, patritis supersedendum discordiis,
patriae nouum temptandum iter decreueritis.'

Mulierem uobis praesento tam ciuibus commendatam suis quam
omnibus exteris admirabilem, Reipublicae Hibernicae Praesidem,

MARIAM ROBINSON

N OR *law, nor duty bade me fight,*
Nor public men, nor cheering crowds.

How apt these words of Yeats for the woman we honour, who has brought such freshness of purpose to Irish politics, and has scattered the ranks of faction and party, and signals a new era of political change and social reform. She was educated at Trinity College, Dublin, and the Harvard Law School, and returned to Trinity to become at the age of twenty-five its youngest ever Professor of Law. A year later she was elected to one of the College's seats in the Upper House of Parliament and so became her country's youngest Senator. Combining the roles of wife, mother of three children, teacher, politician, and barrister, she achieved a commanding reputation as a champion of liberal causes, of the rights of women, minorities, and the underprivileged, and often took her battles against the established laws to the European Courts of Justice and Human Rights. Twice, as candidate of the Labour Party, she sought election to the Lower House, and twice was defeated. Undaunted, she sought a yet greater prize. As an independent candidate, beginning as a 100–1 outsider, she visited every city, town, and village, and every inhabited island, and was elected to the highest office 'by men and women' (to quote her own words) 'of all parties and none, by many with great moral courage who stepped out from the faded flags of the civil war and voted for a new Ireland'.

I present to you a woman who has captured the minds of her compatriots and the admiration of the world,

MARY ROBINSON,

President of Ireland.

ΑΓΕΩΜΕΤΡΗΤΟΣ ΜΗΔΕΙΣ ΕΙΣΙΤΩ. nouistis Academiae Platonis inscriptionem. sed non equidem, ita me di ament, uolo profanum uulgus arcere: nam de numerorum θεωρίαι, de probabilitatis calculo, de combinandi μεθόδωι, de formularum graphicarum εἰκαιότητι, de ἀcυνθέτων argumento simplici, cum fidenter nesciam disputare, non haec est occasio disputandi. de ipso tamen homine fabulari licet: quippe fabula est, non homo. Aristotelem περιπάτοιc exsuperat, modo huc it, modo illuc, ubiuis terrarum semper uolat: nam *mobilitate uiget* discipulosque *adquirit eundo*. puta quouis gentium hunc auolasse. omnia quae possidet (nam non possidentem multa recte beatum uocat) in unica secum adportat mantica, nisi quod aenigmatum supellectili praemunitus est quibus titillet hospites. 'sunt hic etiam sua praemia' nuntiat (nam aenigmata soluentes praemiis munerat), tum 'patet nostri ianua cerebri' uel 'alterum πρόβημα, alterum πρόβλημα' (nam Pythico ritu solet loqui). est iugis inuentionis fons, mathematicorum qui ubique sunt deliciae: nonne commentariola amplius mille et trecenta conscripsit, mathematicos amplius ducentos quinquaginta scribendi consortes habet? et quamquam uniuersi mundi ciuis est, praecipuo beneficii mutui uinculo cum nobis copulatur. quid si ab inferis testes aduocem manes fabulosos, doctorum par nobile, te, Robuste, te, Siluicule, qui hunc iuniorem hospitiis uestris exceperistis? sed uos satius sit obtestari, Consocii superstites, qui hunc hospitis iure Socium quondam creauistis, huius natales cum septuagesimos tum quintos septuagesimos commentariis corrogatis et conuiuiorum festiuitate celebrastis.

Praesento uobis ex Academiae Scientiarum Hungaricae Instituto Mathematico, Societatis Regiae iure peregrino Sodalem,

PAVLVM ERDÖS

'KEEP OUT: *Mathematicians Only' said the notice affixed to Plato's Academy. But do not depart, or close your ears. About number theory, the probabilistic method, combinatorics, random graphs, or the Elementary Proof of the Prime Number Theorem, I shall not discourse, for I cannot discourse with conviction. But, if I cannot speak of the subjects in which his genius is acknowledged, without pretence I can speak of the man himself, of whom legends are told, and all of those legends are true. He has never held a permanent post. He is the most peripatetic scholar since Aristotle, and he never stops moving but flies hither and thither, wherever he can find a welcome – and he can find a welcome everywhere. He arrives, with all he owns in a suitcase (for he considers private property a nuisance) and with a bundle of elegant ready-made problems, offering prizes to those who can help him to solve them. 'Here I am: my brain is open', or 'Another roof: another proof' – for he speaks in a style the Delphic priestess would admire. You may gauge his fertility in invention, and the devotion of fellow mathematicians, from this: he has written more than 1300 papers, with more than 250 co-authors. Although he is a citizen of the world, he is bound to Cambridge by long-standing ties of mutual affection, for here in his youth our own legends, Hardy and Littlewood, welcomed him, and here half a century later he is still the most fêted of guests. He has been a Visiting Fellow Commoner of Trinity, and our colleagues celebrated both his seventieth and his seventy-fifth birthdays with banquets and Festchriften.*

I present to you

PAUL ERDÖS,

of the Mathematical Institute of the Hungarian Academy of Sciences, Foreign Member of the Royal Society.

'VNVS quisque homo non unam, dum transit aetatem, personam sustinet.' sed hic quis, quaeso, in nostrum procedit theatrum? num adcessit Herbertus, ingenui uultus puer, an Iudaeus paedagogus, citra humanitatem homo? num Gulleius, Apellis instar, nisi quod gradum dissolutum trahit et non uocem remittit sed gargalizationem, an Carolus, eius nominis primus, carnifici praebens caput, rex ad unguem regius? num imperator Eous, qui inuictam fortitudinem summa cum temeritate confusit, an Scoticae cohortis Pyrgopolinices, commissationibus impotentiam contegens, mendax umbra militis?

ede quid illum
esse putes: quemuis hominem secum adtulit ad nos.

Atellanarum nempe meministis. nam cui non notus Henricus, argentariorum minister, modestia superans Catonem, Autolycum furacitate? cui non Marcus mouit cachinnos, harpagonum choragus, latronis assuetior quam lyristae modis? hic e gente Asconiana non unam Agatham tantummodo egit, suffragatricem praenobilem, sed Diti deditam, di magni, octuplam omnem propaginem. idem, siquando cothurno commutat socculum, admirationem uel maiorem colligit, siue gregarii militis, nomine mutato Rossii, ingenium multiplex detegit, siue Gulielmum inducit senem, infractum decoctorum patronum, siue Georgium, speculatorum speculatorem, parco sermone depingit. nec te, gladiator intermundiorum, praeteribo. nam cum ensem fulminantem coruscas, quis tibi non puerulorum manibus complosis adstrepit? ne plura: est in conspectu uir tam uitae quam artis interpres, uiuidam cuius artem non fuga temporum diruet.

Praesento uobis Equitem Auratum, Excellentissimi Ordinis Imperii Britannici Commendatorem,

ALEC GUINNESS

'A<small>ND</small> *one man in his time plays many parts*'.[1]

But who is this who now steps forth on to our stage? Is it innocent merry-eyed Herbert Pocket, or Fagin, fiendish pedagogue? Is it Gulley Jimson, with shuffling gait and gargle of a voice, or Charles I, ascending the scaffold every inch a King? Is it tight-lipped Colonel Nicholson, heroic in folly, or loud swaggering Lt-Colonel Jock Sinclair?

> *A man so various that he seems to be*
> *Not one, but all mankind's epitome.*[2]

In younger years he gave us the broad comic roles: Henry Holland, bowler-hatted bank clerk, meek-mannered mobster of Lavender Hill, Professor Marcus, bogus musician with a cello-case of loot, Lady Agatha, suffragette, and the whole doomed dynasty of d'Ascoynes. And then he showed us the enigma of Private Ross, the fallible dignity of William Dorritt, Father of the Marshalsea, and silent solitary spycatcher Smiley. And he has found yet a new generation of admirers, as sage of the galaxies, last of the Jedi knights, Ben Kenobi, lord of the laser sword. Age cannot wither him nor custom stale his infinite variety. He is a maker of images inimitable, imperishable, a performer of the highest art, which seems not art at all but life.

I present to you

Sir ALEC GUINNESS, C.B.E.

[1] Shakespeare. *As You Like It*, II. vii. 142.
[2] Dryden, *Absalom and Achitophel*, Part I, 545–6. The Latin speech quotes Juvenal, 3. 74–5.

HAEC ciuitati summa libertas, ubi
e publica re proloqui quiuis potest;
qui uult, probatur; qui secus, lingua fauet;
his aequius quid fiat aut honestius?

Adest qui libere mauult loqui quam uultum instantis tyranni uel ciuium ardorem praua iubentium pertimescere. ob carmen puerile ludo expulsus est, propter religionem et in actis diurnis commentarios tyrannis odiosus patriam profugit, ardua montium pede transgressus Slouakiam petiit, Hesperiam amplexus Transatlanticam studia re-sumpsit intermissa et copiis libertatis Europaeae uindicibus adscriptus non sine gloria militauit. bello confecto ad patriam redux ingenio ultra legem liberali, stilo salso subtili subdolo, oestri cuiusdam instar uernaculi, magistratuum maleficia pergebat pungere. libros itinera contiones lex coercebat, coercere uocem non ualebat. scripta tum conciues tum homines exteri postulant lectitant adprobant. quid *Crucesignatos* praedicem, quid *Iudaeum Circumuagum*, quid *Dauidis Regis Commentariolum*? en apologos omni laude maiores, en aere omni perenniora monumenta. uitae gloriosae summam gloriam adtendite: qui admodum iuuenis Berolini seruitutem pati recusauerat, idem aetate prouectus muri monstrum Berolinensis a ciuibus seruitutis impatientibus uidit euersum, euersi ruinas inter primos transiit, libertatis restitutae praesens nuntius.

Praesento uobis litterarum Germanicarum decus, libertatis atque liberalitatis Germanicae propugnaculum,

STEPHANVM HEYM

> T HIS *is true liberty when free-born men*
> *Having to advise the public may speak free,*
> *Which he who can, and will, deserves high praise,*
> *Who neither can nor will, may hold his peace;*
> *What can be juster in a state than this?*[1]

Here is a man who has chosen to speak freely, whose purpose is not shaken by 'the tyrant's lowering countenance' or 'the zeal of countrymen commanding wrong'. He was expelled from school because of a poem, and became a fugitive from his country because of his religion and his journalism. He escaped arrest by flight on foot through the mountains to Czechoslovakia, completed his education in America, served with the US forces in Europe, and was decorated for bravery. He returned to East Germany, and, although his liberal ideals found no favour, he remained, to be a gadfly to successive administrations, satirising in his fiction and exposing in his newspaper columns the inefficiency, corruption, and hypocrisy of government. Often forbidden to publish, travel, or address public meetings, he none the less established a commanding name in his country and outside, through such novels as The Crusaders, *and* The Wandering Jew, *and* The King David Report, *all of them best-sellers in many languages. And when the Berlin Wall was breached, he, who had begun his fight against tyranny in that city while yet a mere youth, now, an old man, was first among those who stepped through the wall to proclaim that liberty had returned to his land.*

For his unique contribution to German literature, and for the inspiration which he has given to the people of East Germany in their progress towards democracy, we honour

STEFAN HEYM

---

[1] Euripides, *Suppliant Women*, 438–41, prefixed by Milton to his *Areopagitica: For the Liberty of Unlicensed Printing*. The English translation is Milton's. The following sentence alludes to Horace, *Odes*, 3.3.

CVM Christophoro Wren ultimum hunc hospitem uinculo quodam necessitudinis esse coniunctum quis neget? uidelicet Vrbem reconcinnandam curauit ille uastatam incendio, hic duello. huius industriam Londiniensem probant scholae domicilia aedificia sescenta, probat ore nescio an facundiore Festiuitatis Aula Regalis. postquam ad nos arcessitus est, ut Architecturae Professor omnium primus crearetur, plurima nobis ingenii sui pignora reliquit. nonne Institutum indagationibus deditum condidit, quod beneficii memores Martinum nuncupauimus? nonne huius ductu atque auspiciis simul schola Cantabrigiensis inclarescere, simul uniuersa ciuitas nouas institutionis architectonicae disciplinas ingredi coepit? huius si monumentum requiritur,

> laudabunt alii claris pictoribus aptam
> quis Olisipo superbiat aulam,
> aut odea tuis, urbs o Glasgouia, Musis
> digna Caledonioque cothurno,
> aut Academias et conuiualibus aulis
> insignes et bibliothecis.
> me, Camus lentis ubi praeterlabitur undis,
> delectat domus Harueiana,
> me noua Kettleiae superaddita porticus aulae
> et schola Melpomenes numerosa,
> et prope consurgens, uersae miracula formae,
> antiquo confinia quondam
> horrea pistrino, iam nunc spectabilis aedes,
> grata tuis, Shelfordia, nymphis.

Praesento uobis Equitem Auratum, Magistrum in Artibus, Collegii Iesu Socium emeritum et honoris causa Socium creatum, Architecturae Professorem emeritum, Academiae Regiae adscriptum, Instituti Regalis Architectorum Britannicorum aureo nomismate ornatum,

IOHANNEM LESLEIVM MARTIN

A FTER *the Great Fire the citizens of London turned to Sir Christopher Wren. Three centuries later, after the devastations of war, they turned to our honorand, Deputy and then Chief Architect to the London County Council. The schools and houses whose building he planned are now the silent fabric of the city. The Royal Festival Hall speaks forth in more eloquent witness. We welcomed him to Cambridge as our first Professor of Architecture, and he founded the research centre now named in his honour as the Martin Centre for Architectural and Urban Studies, and he placed Cambridge in the forefront of architectural teaching and research, and at the same time changed the whole direction of architectural education in the country. Some, if they seek his monument, may find it in Lisbon, where he has designed the Gallery of Contemporary Art; others in Glasgow, where he built a new home for the Royal Scottish Academy of Music and Drama; others in the libraries, auditoria, and halls of residence with which he has enriched many a University. But you and I will find it beside the Cam, in Harvey Court of Caius, or in the Gallery of Kettle's Yard, or in the Music School, whose concert hall has earned the applause of listener and performer alike; or by the banks of the millpond at Great Shelford, where he has converted the old mill and barn into his studio and home.*

I present to you

Sir JOHN LESLIE MARTIN, M.A.,

Emeritus Fellow and Honorary Fellow of Jesus College, Emeritus Professor of Architecture, Royal Academician, gold medallist of the Royal Institute of British Architects.

ADEST qui Britanniam Henrico eius nominis septimo, mox octauo, post Elizabethae regnatam nouis distinxit coloribus. adest qui in hac stat sententia pertinax, popularis aurae neglegens: esse unam et absolutam in rebus historicis ueritatem, quae non ab historici iudicio sed ab ipsis rebus pendeat, eamque non propterea esse quaerendam quod qui recte praeterita cognoscat rectius praesentia uel futura sit cogniturus sed quod inquisitio ueri sit opus sincerum ingenuum prorsus humanum, suam habens in se satisfactionem. nonne ueram personam Thomae Cromwell reddidit? en e Seiano factum Solonem, en incorruptum ministrum, en legum latorem prouidum. at quantas adcendit controuersias! quantum flammis oleum superaddidit! cetera quis nescit uolumina? amplius uiginti contexuit libros, quorum hos duo, *Europa Reformata* et *Britanniae Tudorianae Tempora*, nemo tironum nostrorum non diurna, non nocturna uersat manu. quid quod edicta de recta historiae conscribendae ratione proferre non desinit? quot turbas facit peruersa manu Clio tractantibus! ite hinc socioanthropopsychologissantium cateruae! ne illos quidem, quippe quorum laus in oratione ponatur, Gibbonium Clarendonium Macauleium, maioris aestimat. quid? nullius magistri iurat in uerba? immo, si quos alios, Bartholdum Niebuhr et Leopoldum Ranke magistros habet, utpote unicam ueritatis uiam consecutos, qui e monumentis singula conquirerent, e singulis uniuersa concluderent. habet etiam Fridericum Maitland, quem tali praedicauit commendatione qualis in ipsum iure referatur: 'ex hoc pendet huius uirtus uiri, quod monumenta comprendere, quid possint dicere, quid secus, omnibus neruis enisus est.' restat ut discipulorum, quorum calculus subduci non potest, praeceptorem laudemus singularem. quos quam firmis sibi caritatis uinculis adstrinxerit testatur commentariorum natales celebrantium quinquiens oblata pietas.

Praesento uobis Equitem Auratum, Doctorem in Litteris, Academiae Britannicae Sodalem, Collegii de Clare Socium, Aeui Recentioris Regium Professorem Emeritum,

GALFRIDVM RVDOLPHVM ELTON

HERE *is a historian who, in the course of transforming our perception of Tudor England, has preached and practised with unswerving conviction and passion an unfashionable doctrine: that there is such a thing as objective truth about the past, and that this truth is worthy to be sought and studied not for its relevance to the present or the future but for its own sake and on its own terms and in its own right. He began by rehabilitating Thomas Cromwell, and recast the traditional dark agent of Tudor despotism in the new role of lawmaker and administrator of genius, who amended the processes of government and the structure of the state and made the Reformation a reality. He ignited a controversy which still blazes, and to which from time to time he has added new fuel. The sum of his writings is more than twenty volumes, and among these especial praise may be accorded to those imposing textbooks which all undergraduates and sixth-formers swear by,* England under the Tudors *and* Reformation Europe. *But let us not omit his periodic disquisitions on the historian's craft, in which he routs the ranks of unbelievers. To sociologizing, anthropologizing, psychologizing historians he gives no quarter. By Gibbon, Clarendon, and Macaulay, 'whose readability is their main claim to fame', he is not moved. His masters are the great nineteenth-century German historians, such as Niebuhr and Ranke, who pursued the one true historical method, 'which grounds detail upon evidence and generalization upon detail', or F. W. Maitland, of whom he has said, what may be said of him, that 'the mainstay of his strength lay in his determination to understand his sources – their contents and their limitations'. The devotion with which he has nurtured generations of graduate students has passed into legend, and the veneration in which he is held by them has found public expression in no fewer than five Festschriften which have marked his anniversaries.*

I present to you

Sir GEOFFREY RUDOLPH ELTON, LITT.D., F.B.A.,

Fellow of Clare College, Regius Professor Emeritus of Modern History.

N E temptare Deum, ne qui sit nosse rogando
quaesieris: hominem noscere quaerat homo.

Abhinc annos quadraginta adulescens ab Italia profectus, dum in elaboratorio Ronaldi Fisher, uiri βιομαθηματικωτάτου, tirocinii rudimenta ponit, explorationem sibi destinabat omnes audaciae fines supergressam: ut genetiuas hominum particulas examinaret, si forte humanum genus unde terrarum esset oriundum, quibus inde per orbem migrasset semitis comperiret. in Italiam redux a ualle Parmensi fecit exordium: tria saecula permensus genetiuam incolarum conformationem abaco suo computauit. cedunt Parmenses Pygmaeis Africanis, concedit abacus computatrici machinae. at mehercule haec machina, ingenio quamuis praepeti praedita, machinatorem uix adaequat: Pegasus est, non caballus. nam raptim ex omnibus quotquot ubique sunt nationibus particularum genetiuarum notitiam colligit. rudem indigestamque molem materiae, μάψ, ἀτὰρ οὐ κατὰ κόcμον adhuc iacentem, in ordinem redigit et similitudines in diuersitate rimatur. quod olim in uotis erat, nunc ad exitum ducit: ut stemma depingat, quod genus humanum prima ab origine multifidos per ramos ad tempora nostra deductum prae se ferat. o admirabilem genealogorum philologorum archaeologorum consensionem: quippe qui omnes una uoce testentur hominem primigenium in Africa natum, cuius progenies primum in Asiam, mox in Europam, post Australes in insulas, postremo in Americam fluctibus continuatis exundauerit.

Libet hodie piare delicta maiorum, qui, spreta Fisheri sententia, tironem exauctoratum dimiserunt domum. at hic, qua est humanitate, non nobis uitio uertit hanc improuidentiam. nec nos grauari decet, si tot cum nationibus noster sit nobis communicandus. nam reapse, quod ex ipsius inuentis patet, sumus omnes unius una pars nationis.

Praesento uobis Magistrum in Artibus, Collegii Gonuillii et Caii honoris causa Socium, in Vniuersitate Stanfordiensi Genetices Professorem,

LVDOVICVM LVCAM CAVALLI-SFORZA

K NOW *then thyself, presume not God to scan:*
The proper study of mankind is man.[1]

Forty years ago, when he was studying bacteriology in the laboratory of Sir Ronald Fisher in Cambridge, a young biochemist formulated a project of unbelievable boldness and ambition: to determine, from a study of the genes, in what part of the globe the human race originated, and to trace the paths by which it spread throughout the world. He reasoned that this task might be accomplished by mapping the distribution of individual genes in all existing populations. Returning to his native Italy, he began his quest in the Parma valley, where, with the aid of primitive punched-card tabulators, he examined the genetic structure of the people of that region during the last three centuries. He moved to the Pygmies of Africa, whose genes take us closer to our earliest ancestor. And, as the ever-increasing power and speed of the computer sought to keep pace with the Horse-Power of the man, he mapped the distribution of hundreds of genes in thousands of populations worldwide, and he looked for patterns in those maps. And so the science of phylogenetics was born, and the family tree of which he had dreamed spread forth its branches, which trace the descent of man from the first creation. What the geneticist discovered, the linguist and archaeologist confirm. For genes and stones and tongues now speak with one voice: they speak of a man born in Africa, whose progeny spread, by wave after wave of migration, first to Asia and then to Europe and then to the Pacific and the New World.

Today we right an ancient wrong. For Fisher requested that his pupil should be promoted to the office of Assistant Director of Research. If that request had been granted, we might not have had to share him with so many other nations. But he does not hold it against us, for he is the most generous and warm-hearted of men. And, as he has taught us, we are all in truth one nation.

I present to you

LUIGI LUCA CAVALLI-SFORZA, M.A.,

Honorary Fellow of Gonville and Caius College, Professor of Genetics, Stanford University.

---

[1] Pope, *An Essay on Man, Epistle* 2, 1–2.

E RAT unus Argonautarum Lynceus, qui

ὀξυτάτοιϲ ἐκέκαϲτο
ὄμμαϲιν, εἰ ἐτεόν γε πέλει κλέοϲ ἀνέρα κεῖνον
ῥηιδίωϲ καὶ νέρθεν ὑπὸ χθονὸϲ αὐγάζεϲθαι.[1]

fidem fictis addidit Roentgenus, non ita tamen ut cerebri cauernas illuminaret. uenit hic noster, machinae computatricis inuentor, et alteram machinatur inuentionem uel magis callidam et CATam.

> protinu' molitur radiorum lucida tela
> atque ea continuo cursu circum omne cerebrum
> circumagit ex alioque alium transducit in axem,
> totius capitis templa omnia circumlustrans.
> contemplator enim, cum lux extraria portas
> perfringit cerebri et transit penetralia et exit
> inde per oppositos postes: corpuscula lucis
> sunt emissa foras non omnia uiribus aequis,
> propterea quia, quae per tenuia cumque cerebri
> texta meant, mage procliuis datur exitus ollis,
> at contra, quibus est obiectus materiai
> densior, obtundunt uires marcentque meando.
> uix mora, colescunt iterum et, prout cuique superstat
> uis sua, disparibus formis et dispare filo
> in simulacra ruunt perlustratique cerebri
> singula conseruant uestigia particulatim,
> ut, tamquam in speculo uideas, dinoscere possis
> quae sit texturae distantia differitasque.
> quod superest, si consimili ratione uelis quem
> totum hominem et corpus totum scrutarier, omnis
> intestinorum circumcaesura patescit.
> usque adeo hic ualuit cum leni luminis ictu
> chirurgi fregisse minas ferrumque tremendum.

Praesento uobis Equitem Auratum, Excellentissimi Ordinis Imperii Britannici Commendatorem, Regiae Societatis Sodalem, laureis Nobelianis coronatum, diu in elaboratoriis Thornianis EMInentem,

GODOFREDVM NEWBOLD HOUNSFIELD

[1] Apollonius Rhodius, *Argonautica*, 1.153–5.

T HERE *was an Argonaut called Lynceus,*

> *With eyes so sharp, if legend be believed,*
> *That he could look into the very earth*
> *And bring to light the caverns of the deep.*

When Roentgen invented X-rays in 1895, he transformed legend into science. But the caverns of the human brain remained in darkness, until our honorand arrived to illumine them. He had already invented the first solid-state computer to be built in Great Britain, and he harnessed the power of the computer to the service of medicine, by inventing computerized axial tomography, which the world now knows by the friendlier name of CAT. He caused a narrow X-ray beam to traverse the brain and slowly to describe a full circle around it. He repeated the procedure on successive planes, until the whole brain had been scanned. The beam, as it passes through the brain, is absorbed by the tissues in greater or lesser degree, in proportion to their density, and, when it emerges, its remaining strength is measured at every point. This information, when processed by computer, is displayed on a television screen as a succession of images, in which the subtlest differences in the tissues of the brain are revealed with miraculous clarity. Using the same technique, he developed the body-scanner. So that now we may look at the internal organs without recourse to the surgeon's exploratory knife.

I present to you a Nobel laureate, who has revolutionized the detection, diagnosis, and treatment of disease,

Sir GODFREY NEWBOLD HOUNSFIELD, C.B.E., F.R.S.,

Consultant, Thorn EMI Central Research Laboratories.

ANNOS abhinc triginta famae fundamenta iecit hospes hic noster, cum Edmundi Husserl disputationem *De Geometriae Principiis* praefatione copiosa recensuit. exinde perenni tamquam fonte innumerabilem commentariorum seriem et libros amplius uiginti profudit, quorum alii, uelut Περὶ Γραμματολογίας et Τὸ ἐν Γραφῆι Διάφορον, austeram frontem, alii, quales sunt Ὠτοβιογραφίαι et *Chartulae* Cωκρατικοφροιδιάζουσαι, paene ridibundam prae se ferunt. sed *deridentem dicere uerum quid uetat?*[1] ut qui ingenium nullo limite circumscriptum exerceat, immo philologiae philosophiae psychologiae adfinitates uno simul complectatur obtutu, nonne dignus est qui caelesti illi sophistarum Francogallorum coetui inseratur qui inde a Dionysio Diderot deinceps floruerunt? quid quod omnes omnium usque ab ipso Platone sapientium de ueritate doctrinas lance, ne dicam naso, gaudet suspendere? nam philosophorum fidem, si qui unam et absolutam de rebus ueritatem cogitatione sectantur, lectorum fidem, si qui simplicem dumtaxat et unum sensum in sermone rimantur, explodit exturbat exsibilat. nam non ea tantum quae aut dicta aut scripta sunt examinando sed etiam indicta aut inter se contraria deprehendendo, sicut Ouidius alter, *sermonem agnoscit quod non uideatur agentem.*[2] nullus enim sermo non alterum sermonem tamquam post siparia delitescentem habet, qui, simul atque in scaenam productus est, tertio partes debet cedere. omnis nimirum oratio contra frenos oratoris repugnat et, si quid est usquam sincerae ueritatis, hoc nemo quamuis diligens orator possit repraesentare. sunt qui huius scripta φωνάεντα cυνετοῖcιν dicere et ἑρμανέων χατίζειν arbitrentur. sunt qui controuersias ab hoc suscitatas aegre ferant. sed numquid citra controuersiam recte potest excuti? nonne τὸν ἀνεξέταστον βίον οὐ βιωτὸν ἀνθρώπωι dixit Socrates?[3]

Praesento uobis uirum ingenio uiuido praeditum et feraci nouorum, qui *libera per uacuum posuit uestigia princeps,*[4] in Schola Scientiarum Socialium Lutetiana Studiorum Rectorem,

IACOBVM DERRIDA

[1] Cf. Horace, *Satires*, 1.1.24–5.
[2] Ovid, *Amores*, 2.5.19.
[3] Plato, *Apology*, 38a.
[4] Horace, *Epistles*, 1.19.21.

O U R *honorand laid the foundations of his fame thirty years ago, with a long critical introduction to* The Origin of Geometry *by the German philosopher Edmund Husserl. Since then he has published essays beyond number and more than twenty books, from* Of Grammatology *and* Writing and Difference *to the more playfully entitled* Otobiographies *and* The Postcard from Socrates to Freud and Beyond. *His writings, which encompass literature, linguistics, philosophy, and psychoanalysis, belong to a genre long established in France, and place him among that noble company of* savants *reaching back in unbroken tradition to the time of Diderot. He rejects many of the presuppositions and habits of thought adopted by philosophers from Plato to the present. He calls into question the belief of the philosopher that ultimate metaphysical certainty is discoverable, and the belief of the reader that the written text harbours one single discoverable meaning. He argues that, by exposing the unformulated propositions and the subtle self-contradictions of the writer, we may show that a text is saying something other than what it appears to be saying. The text is thus 'deconstructed' and a new text emerges. But this new text must be examined afresh, and so the process of deconstruction may be continued in an infinite series of readings. For he maintains that language, however conscientiously we use it, has powers which we cannot control; and that language holds up no mirror to the world, offers no reflection of an external timeless truth.* Il n'y a pas de hors-texte – '*there is nothing outside the text*'. *His style, weaving strange spells and stranger spellings, ranges far beyond the orthodox terms of academic discourse. He does not shun controversy, for controversy ensures debate, and in true debate nothing remains unexamined. As Socrates said, that which is unexamined is without meaning.*

I present to you a man who has launched one of the most imaginative ventures in modern thought,

JACQUES DERRIDA,

Directeur d'Etudes, Ecole des Hautes Etudes en Sciences Sociales, Paris.

EN praeclaram fabularum scriptorem quae uitam uixit uinculis tam artis cum patriae temporibus coniunctam et implicatam ut uiuidum et patriae et temporum documentum arte sua creauerit. non sine periculo, non sine gloria militabat, dum Africanorum causas ac iura sustentat, scriptores Africanos patrocinio suo amplectitur, leges Africanis iniquas non submissa uoce uellicat. existimationis primitias propter fabellas oratione concisa narratas consecuta est. subinde aream magis magisque latam ingenio suo uindicans historiarum decem commenticiarum exegit praegrande monumentum. cui nostrum non notus est Hospes Honoratus uel Conseruator ille Rerum, cui non nota Burgeri Filia siue Gens Iulii? ipsum putes Honorium Francogallorum exstare rediuiuum: nam stilo paene Balzaciano uniuersae ciuitatis uota timores iras uoluptates describit depingit delineat. uidelicet dum multigenos Africae Meridionalis perlustrat incolas, siue atri coloris siue albi, siue pauperes siue diuites, tam innocentes quam noxios, tam iniuriis laborantes quam iniurias inferentes, unius cuiusque penitus inuadit in mentem et sensus intimos percipit. non locorum minore quam hominum abundantia, non minus diuersis regionum quam gentium simulacris pinacothecam suam compleuit. nam siue fumum et opes et strepitum Iohannesburgi perambulat, uel pascuorum Transuaaliensium permetitur uastitates, uel casas stramentis ac luto contextas, arbores baobabianas, stagnorum uligines, metalla tum uiua tum deserta uisit, tam luxuriosa inuentionis ubertate utitur ut, tamquam Antaeus, sic telluris ipsa contactu uires suas semper redintegrare uideatur.

Praesento uobis laurea Nobeliana nuper coronatam

NADINE GORDIMER

HERE *is a writer whose life has been shaped by the country and the times in which she has lived, and who, in turn, has shaped her writing into a true and enduring document of her times and her country. A courageous champion of black causes and black writers, an uncompromising critic of her country's unequal laws, she has trodden a lonely and perilous path between art and politics. She won early renown as a writer of short stories. But over the years her canvas has widened, and in an imposing sequence of ten novels, among them* A Guest of Honour (*James Tait Black Prize, 1972*), The Conservationist (*Booker Prize, 1974*), Burger's Daughter (*1979*), *and* July's People (*1981*), *she has painted, like a modern Balzac, a grand panorama of a whole society. She looks deep into the minds and into the very hearts of the South African people, poor and rich, black and white, innocent and guilty, oppressed and oppressor. Her places are no less diverse than her people. She moves from the noisy streets of Johannesburg to the vastness of the Transvaal veld, to tribal huts and baobab trees and oozy swamps and mines still living and mines abandoned, and her imagination, like the might of the wrestler Antaeus which was ever renewed by contact with the earth, gains ever new strength from the land about her.*

I present to you

NADINE GORDIMER,

Nobel Laureate.

QVI Summi inter Nationes Iudicii fundamenta iecerunt prudenter de iudicibus seligendis cauebant: 'seligatur qui et sit optime moratus et se in iuribus gentium tractandis iurisconsultum sollertem probauerit.' adest iudex omnibus numeris acceptus. num mores quaeruntur optimi? Collegii Iesu Tutor Maximus electus est. de sollertia quaeritur? in componendis inter gentes controuersiis summum se aduocatum et arbitrum praestitit, qui doctrinam humanitate, suadelam comitate condiret. si de scriptis quaesiueris, liber *De finibus secundum ius gentium occupandis* commendationem collegit singularem. magnum existimationi suae cumulum nuper addidit cum notissimum illum librum Oppenheimianum, qui totam de iure gentium doctrinam complectitur, longo situ languentem et paene exoletum, denuo in lucem edidit amplissimis doctrinae incrementis adauctum. mehercule, dum cadis uetustis uinum nouum infundit, Opimianum ex Oppenheim fecit. adcedit quod in Comitatu Eboracensi natus est: unde pendet ardor certaminis quod cum pila clauaque luditur. ergo quid mirum si a comitibus Hagensibus primipilus, quid mirum si claui iudicialis rector creatus est? et medius fidius talem cum iudicem suspicio in Olympo suo editum, iudicum coetu stipatum paene caelesti, repente fit e iudice Iuppiter, qui

> duas aequato examine lances
> sustinet et fata imponit diuersa duorum.[1]

quod si, qua est temperantia, tam sublime detrectat praeconium, paullo minora canamus, Dominum illum Cancellarium inducentes palliatum:

> Consessus ille quem uidetis, hospites,
> est uniuersae exemplar excellentiae:
> et ille iudex iudicum unus omnium
> probissimorum exemplar est probissimum.

Praesento uobis Equitem Auratum, Magistrum in Artibus, Baccalaureum in Iure, Collegiorum Downingiani et Iesu honoris causa Socium, Iuris Gentium Professorem Whewellianum emeritum, Summi inter Nationes Iudicii Praesidem,

ROBERTVM YEWDALL JENNINGS

[1] Vergil, *Aeneid*, 12. 725–6.

THE *founding Statute of the International Court of Justice prescribes that its fifteen members shall be elected 'from among persons of high moral character who ... are jurisconsults of recognized competence in international law.' If you ask for proof of the high moral character of our honorand, was he not Senior Tutor of Jesus? And has he not proved himself a consummate counsel in international disputes and arbitrations, an advocate who combines uncommon learning with a fund of common sense, and rare persuasiveness with scrupulous tact and courtesy? His first book said the last word on* The Acquisition of Territory in International Law. *And, to set the seal on his reputation, he has recently published the ninth edition of* Oppenheim's International Law, *pouring new wine into old bottles by distilling the lore of 37 years since the eighth edition. A vintage performance, if ever there was. He is also a Yorkshireman, which may explain his passion for cricket. And his team-mates at The Hague, when they selected him as Captain, recognised in him a good all-rounder, a straight bat and a safe pair of hands. When I contemplate him, sitting in Olympian eminence, surrounded by a pantheon of judicial deities, I am tempted to compare him to that other President of the Immortals,*

> *Who holds aloft the finely balanced scales*
> *And sets in either pan the rival claims.*

But if he deprecates so august a comparison, since he is a man of great modesty, let me praise him not with the epic voice of Mantua but with the humbler strains of Savoy:

> *The Court's the true embodiment*
> *Of everything that's excellent:*
> *It has no kind of fault or tort,*
> *And he, my Lords, embodies the Court.*

I present to you

Sir ROBERT YEWDALL JENNINGS, M.A., LL.B.,

Honorary Fellow of Downing and Jesus Colleges, Emeritus Whewell Professor of International Law, President of the International Court of Justice.

'ANTIQVAM exquirite matrem' Aeneae profugo dixit oraculum.[1] hic ille est qui Almam suam Matrem iniussus expetit et ab illo usque die quo nomen in matriculam rettulit altera pro matre ducit, qui gratiam cum millesimo rependit non praesenti quidem pecunia sed amoris impensi, obseruantiae singularis munere, qui denique, nouissimum animi pignus, filios duos in iure instruendos fidei nostrae commisit. arbitrio suo argentariam facit, aliorum suffragiis rem publicam capessit, tum in senatum suum electus tum a Seribus proximis consultor ascitus. idem mercator et negotiator impiger commercio inter Asiam et Europam nimium quantum profuit. si quando a tot negotiis otiatur quibus erat ne Hercules quidem suffecturus, artibus litteris causis sescentis promouendis libenter incumbit. honore nostro dignus est, si nil addatur his laudibus. at restat hoc aliud non silendum, quod hunc cum nobis copula uel firmiore coniungit. huius ductu et auspiciis fundata est Amicorum Consortio, quae magnum stipium aceruum pergebat corradere corrasumque iuuenibus qui apud nos instituerentur expendere. Cancellarius ipse noster, qua est beneuolentia, coeptis adnuit. et per annos hos undecim iuuenes sexaginta duos excepimus, 'acceptos, regale nomisma, Philippos' cum se ferentes,[2] qui successu tam incomparabili studia nauauerunt ut quantam ad se ipsos gloriam, tantam ad Cancellarium et hospitem nostrum contulisse uideantur.

Praesento uobis uirum honorabilem, Excellentissimo Ordini Imperii Britannici adscriptum, Pacis Iustitiarium, Magistrum in Artibus, Collegiorum Selwyniani et Robinsoniani honoris causa Socium, Argentariae Asiae Orientalis Rectorem, Consortionis Amicorum Academiae Cantabrigiensis in Ciuitate Hong Kong Praesidem,

DAVID KWOK PO LI

[1] Vergil, *Aeneid*, 3. 96.
[2] Horace, *Epistles*, 2. 1. 234.

'SEEK out your ancient mother,' said the oracle to Aeneas as he wandered homeless from the sack of Troy. Here is a man who needs the prompting of no oracle to seek out his Alma Mater. For, from the day of his matriculation, he has regarded Cambridge as his second home. And he has repaid what he counts to be his debts to us a thousand times over, not in the cold currency of cash but in a fund, more warm and more valuable by far, of deepest affection and of selfless service, and he has lately created a further trust, by placing in our care his two sons, who are reading Law. He is a banker by profession, a politician by the choice of others. He is not only a member of the Legislative Council of Hong Kong but also Adviser on Hong Kong Affairs to the People's Republic of China. As Director of companies almost beyond number, he has brought western trade and business to the East. In the midst of such diversity as would tax the talents of half a dozen men, he is a patron, second to none, of the arts, education, and a multitude of charitable causes. The distinction which he has achieved and the services which he has rendered in his own community would be reason enough why we should honour him today. But still it remains to recall one cause which is dear to his heart, and which binds him to us by a yet more special bond. The Friends of Cambridge University in Hong Kong, founded by his initiative, established a Scholarship Fund, to which our Chancellor graciously consented that his name should be given. During the past eleven years 56 undergraduates and 6 graduates have arrived here as Prince Philip Scholars. The record of their achievements is uniquely distinguished, and returns due honour to our Chancellor and to our honorand.

I present to you the Honourable

DAVID KWOK PO LI, O.B.E., J.P., M.A.,

Honorary Fellow of Selwyn and Robinson Colleges, Director and Chief Executive of the Bank of East Asia Ltd, Chairman of the Hong Kong Friends of Cambridge University.

QVONDAM hospiti nostro matutinum hoc opus erat, machinam ueternosam e somno excitare, quae praepotenti lampadi uires subministraret. ad hanc enim particulas quasdam quae tum creantur cum molecula magno luminis tormento uerberata confringitur una cum Professore suo, Ronaldo Norrish, incassum speculari studebat. mox ob alteram lampada, cum defecisset prior, comparandam emissus instrumentum offendit a militibus aeriis adhibitum, quod hostium regiones noctu latentes praesentaneo fulguris impetu lustraret lustratasque arte photographica describeret. ʻΗὔρηκαʼ clamauit, subito percussus ingeni lumine: ʻnon lucis impetu continenti sed continuatis fulguris pulsibus praeda capietur. quid enim? nonne olim nauiculas submersas pulsuum continua ratione praedari contigit?ʼ inde est ars illa inuenta quae φωτόλυσις nuncupatur, laureis Nobelianis confestim coronanda. mox, ne lumen officinae saeptis circumcluderetur, in pulpito publico inclaruit. puerorum puellarumque multitudines in Theatro Scientiarum Londiniensi fascinauit, dum speciosa promit miracula, artibus illis adhuc potens quas pridem apud nos in ludicris Gilbertianis exprompserat. tunc inTVentium turbam deuinxit domesticam, dum Principiorum Clinamina et Lucida Tela Diei quae sint interpretatur uel iuniores de scientia physica optime meritos praemiis adficit. quid quod nuper incepit quaerere num uis solis in usus nostros possit accommodari? ab his inuestigationibus si quando uacat, in scaenam procedens uel magis gloriosam coram Proceribus contionatur, huius propositi pertinax, nisi disciplinae naturales maioris aestimentur iuuentuti nostrae prorsus deesse rempublicam.

Praesento uobis uirum admodum honorabilem, Ordini insigniter Meritorum adscitum, Doctorem in Scientiis, Collegii Emmanuelis honoris causa Socium, olim Instituti Regii Rectorem et Societatis Regiae Praesidem, in Collegio Imperiali Professorem,

GEORGIVM Baronem PORTER de LUDDENHAM

THERE *was a time when our honorand's first task, on arriving for work, was to start up an old diesel engine on the back of a lorry parked outside the Cavendish. This powered a gigantic searchlight with which his Professor, R.G.W. Norrish, was vainly trying to catch sight of 'free radicals', the highly reactive fragments which are created when a molecule is broken apart under the bombardment of an intensely powerful beam of light. One day the searchlight failed, and he was sent out to find a replacement. He found a flash unit used for taking wartime reconnaissance pictures. And in a flash he had the answer. Realising that the quarry would never be caught by a continuous beam, and remembering the pulse-techniques of radar which he had learned while chasing U-boats, he attacked his prey with brief pulses of intense energy, the first of which created the free radical, while successive pulses, at intervals of less than a millionth of a second, recorded the stages of its transient life. And so the technique of flash photolysis was born, and won for its inventors a Nobel Prize. Soon he accepted the leading role at the 'London Repertory Theatre of Science', the name which he himself once gave to The Royal Institution. Here schoolchildren flocked in their thousands to see and hear his spectacular lectures, in which he proved that science and showmanship are not incompatible, displaying a talent already familiar to those who had seen his Gilbert and Sullivan performances at Cambridge. The nation at large saw him too on the smaller screen, expounding the* Laws of Disorder *and the* Natural History of a Sunbeam *and as host for fifteen years to* The Young Scientist of the Year. *Even now, when he is not in his laboratory, studying the benefits of solar energy, he may be heard lecturing our legislators on the need for greater investment in scientific education, in a yet grander theatre, the Upper House.*

I present to you the Right Honourable

GEORGE Baron PORTER of LUDDENHAM, O.M., SC.D.,

Honorary Fellow of Emmanuel College, formerly Director of the Royal Institution and President of the Royal Society, Chairman of the Centre for Photomolecular Sciences, Imperial College, University of London.

ANNI iam sunt amplius centum cum Elizabethae Garrett Anderson, mulieri memoriae sempiternae, Regale Medicorum Collegium occlusit ostium. quae tandem aliquando, doctrinae rudimentis unciatim hinc inde quaesitis, illud impetrauit, quod erat iam nulli nostrarum concessum feminae, ut medicinalem tractaret artem. en alteram feminam alterius facti ducem, quam et ipsam iuuauit insignem petere inde coronam unde prius nulli uelarant tempora medici. in Aula Dominae Margarethae Oxoniensi disciplinae primitias adsecuta, Londinii primum in nosocomio Collegii Vniuersitatis uersata est deinde in Bromptoniano, ubi annos per quindecim medicinae Θωρακικῆς partes professorias agebat. pectoris morbis et potissimum spiritus angustiis sese exercebat medendo et exercitationis prouentus libro auctoritatis differto con-credidit. dum Decanae officio fungitur ad ceteros se natam ducendos praestitit, hereditatem palam testata, Roberto Baden-Powell haud indigna neptis. immo, postquam Conuentus Collegiorum Faculta-tumque Medicarum praesul electa est, Boudiccam rediuiuam putes, quae reipublicae ministros utpote tam medicorum quam aegrotorum saluti damna minitantes omnibus neruis frustrari·niteretur. nimirum, cum a ministrorum primaria in congressum esset arcessita, 'pro durum colloquium!' mussitauit quispiam. 'at illa tantum obduruit' risit alter 'ut par pro pari possit referre nostrae'. Bellonam mitto, Musarum laudo famulam et Gratiarum: nam Apollinem artibus musicis, Apellem pictoriis aemulatur, et morum praebet comitatem omni maiorem praeconio.

Praesento uobis Excellentissimi Ordinis Imperii Britannici Dominam Commendatricem, Regalis Medicorum Collegii Praesidem emeritam,

MARGARETHAM ELIZABETHAM HARVEY
TURNER-WARWICK

A CENTURY *and more ago the Royal College of Physicians barred its doors to Elizabeth Garrett Anderson. At length, after an arduous and piecemeal training, she achieved what no woman had achieved in this country before her, a licence to practise medicine. Here is a second pioneer, the first woman to achieve the highest office which the Royal College of Physicians can bestow. After her undergraduate studies at Lady Margaret Hall, Oxford, she embarked on a clinical career in London and became a specialist in the treatment of diseases of the chest, in particular asthma, at University College Hospital and then at the Brompton Hospital, where she was Professor of Thoracic Medicine for fifteen years. The fruits of her experience are enshrined in an authoritative textbook,* The Immunology of the Lung. *As Dean of the Clinical School she proved herself a natural leader, as one might expect, for she is a grand-niece of Lord Baden-Powell. She also proved herself a veritable Boudicca, when, as Chairman of the Conference of the Medical Royal Colleges and their Faculties, she united the whole medical profession behind her, to hold back the encroaching forces of government, which threatened the health of patients and doctors alike. Once, when she had been summoned to Downing Street, a colleague remarked: 'That will be a tough meeting'. To which another replied: 'Mrs Thatcher is tough enough to cope'. But the Muses and Graces have smiled on her no less than Mars, for she is a skilled musician and painter in watercolours, and her courtesy and charm are lauded by all.*

I present to you

Dame MARGARET ELIZABETH HARVEY TURNER-WARWICK,

Past President of the Royal College of Physicians.

HELIX Gemina, altera molecularum spira alteram implicans, res pulchra et mirabilis harmoniae, omnibus nota est. nec est qui nesciat Helicis exemplar duorum iuuenum studiis concordibus excogitatum e chartularum segmentis et filis ferreis annis abhinc quadraginta non procul ab hac curia esse fabricatum. qua fabricatione omnis patefacta est acidi deoxyribonucleici conformatio. et, cum ex hoc acido creentur corpuscula genetiua, patefactum est hoc aliud, quemadmodum formula genetiua a cellulis custodiatur et prognatae cellulae, postquam una se in duas diuisit, custodienda tradatur. propterea quo possint pacto

> generatim saecla referre
> naturam mores uictum motusque parentum[1]

tandem certa ratione compertum tenemus. uix mirum si praemii Nobeliani partem suam reportauit hospes hic noster. et Bookerianum si reportasset uix foret mirum. quid? nonne de helicis indagatione historiam conscripsit probatissimam? quantam argumenti grauitatem quanta orationis festiuitate temperauit! qui contentionis ardor, quot uel in cauponis doctrinae commercia! a, quotiens cor palpitat, dum hunc riuales praecurrere nitentem ad metam plausibus meis incito! sed quo feror? palmam adeptus ad lares suos reuersus est, in finibus scientiae biologicae propagandis dux futurus et signifer, primum apud Haruardianos postea in Insula Longa uersatus, ubi annos iam uiginti quinque celeberrimi illius elaboratorii praefectus est quod ad portum locatur unde olim ballaenarum piscatores enauigabant. laeti reducem salutamus uirum inter heroas pridem relatum, Iasona alterum aureae praedae petitorem, alterum Oedipum Sphingis domitorem CauendDishiaNAe.

Praesento uobis Collegii de Clare honoris causa Socium, Elaboratorii ad Fontis Frigidi Portum siti Rectorem,

IACOBVM DEWEY WATSON

[1] Lucretius, 1. 597–8.

FORTY *years ago in a laboratory not far from here two young scientists built a model out of cardboard and wire, a thing of beauty and wondrous harmony, a double helix, two spiral chains of chemical molecules intertwined about a common axis. The model revealed the chemical structure of DNA, deoxyribonucleic acid, the substance from which our genes are made. It revealed how the human cell stores the genetic code and, when it divides, transmits that code to the daughter cell, how, in short, heredity is transmitted,*

> *Why each new child, through each new generation,*
> *In aspect, character, and way of life,*
> *Reveals the imprint of its parentage.*

It won them a Nobel Prize. But you might have tipped our honorand for the Booker Prize too, for he narrated the quest for the double helix in a best-seller, a breathless drama salted with mischievous good humour, a race against rivals and time, with inspiration flowing in the Eagle no less than in the Cavendish. Returning to his homeland, he became the guide and standard-bearer for others in varied fields of biological exploration, first at Harvard and then at Long Island, as Director for twenty-five years of that famed community of scientists who live and work and teach by the sea, in buildings, now restored to glorious new life, which have their origins in the whaling era. Let us hasten to welcome home to the scene of his youthful triumphs a Jason who once sailed the Cam in quest of the golden molecule, an Oedipus who once solved the riddle of life in the Cavendish.

I present to you

JAMES DEWEY WATSON,

Honorary Fellow of Clare College, Director of the Cold Spring Harbor Laboratory.

ANNIS abhinc centum et quinquaginta Carolus Babbage, Mathematices Professor Lucasianus, organum ἀναλυτικὸν excogitauit, computatricis machinae quae nunc est proplasma, sed pro materiae copiis quae tunc erant praematurius. adest qui Caroli inuento summam manum imposuit, quippe qui ultimum illud quod in uotis manebat, memoriae facultatem, inuenerit. nempe praecepta machinae tradenda taeniis impressit impressaque in sonos ultra aurium captum acutos conuertit. hos in fistulam hydrargyro refertam inmisit et hydrarguri densitate tardatos in unum perpetuum diaulum circinauit. en nouum productum miraculum, machinam memori mente praeditam, laudibus paene Vergilianis efferendam:

> spiritus EDSAC alit totamque infusa per artus
> mens agitat molem et magno se corpore miscet.[1]

fit undique concursus admirantium. mirantur qui chemicas tractant quaestiones, mirantur qui *caeli meatus radio describunt*. hi statim oraculi tamquam fidem sciscitantes perplexissimas numerorum computationes postulant et responsa non modo Pythiis laureis digna sed etiam Nobelianis reportant. cetera quis nescit ab hoc inuenta? quid loquar μικροπρόγραμμα? quid TITANA? o obsequentem et tractabilem giganta! qui non te cum taeniis extra limen accessus petentem differat sed mandata quae domi conscripseris, qua est bracchiorum proceritate, comprehendat. quid plura? nam disciplinae computatiuae uirtus haec nostra, quam nos gloriamur, aemulantur ceteri, ab hoc uno pendet omnis.

Praesento uobis Magistrum in Artibus, Doctorem in Philosophia, Regiae Societatis Sodalem, Collegii Sancti Iohannis Euangelistae Socium, Technologiae Computatiuae Professorem emeritum,

MAVRITIVM VINCENTIVM WILKES

[1] Vergil, *Aeneid*, 6. 726–7. For the radio-astronomers see 6. 849–50.

A CENTURY *and a half ago Charles Babbage, Lucasian Professor of Mathematics, devised his Analytical Engine, which embodied most of the concepts which we now take for granted in the digital computer. But those concepts were far ahead of the available technology. Here stands the man who finally brought to its fullest reality Babbage's dream, by providing the computer with the one vital organ which it still lacked: a capacious memory. He converted a program and its data, punched onto paper tape, into ultrasonic pulses, and he fed the pulses into a tube of mercury, which delayed their progress, and he caused the pulses to circulate indefinitely. And so EDSAC was born, the Electronic Delay Storage Automatic Calculator, the first fully operational computer with its own memory store. As Virgil almost said,*

> *A spirit nourishes the parts within,*
> *And mind moves matter in the mighty frame.*

From all sides they flocked to admire it, and stayed to use it. Soon it was performing the vital calculations by which our chemists and radio-astronomers perfected their Nobel Prize-winning work. On those glorious pioneering days he has never ceased to build. With EDSAC 2 he introduced the revolutionary concept of the microprogram. With TITAN he took a further giant stride forward, enabling a multitude of users, instead of waiting their turn in a queue with their strip of punched tape, to key in their programs simultaneously from their own desks, at whatever distance. He has given us a computer laboratory which is a source of no small parochial pride and is the admiration and envy of the world outside.

I present to you

MAURICE VINCENT WILKES, M.A., PH.D., F.R.S.,

Fellow of St John's College, Emeritus Professor of Computer Technology.

ERGO Iris croceis per caelum roscida pennis
mille trahens uarios aduerso sole colores
deuolat.[1]

en ab utroque arcus cornu splendent libri philosophici, quorum alter artioribus circumscriptus terminis Iohannis Pauli doctrinas ac somnia recludit, alter filo uberiore deductus *Metaphysica Ethicodidascala* complectitur. in medio locantur fabulae scaenicae, melicorum libellus, sermonum Platonicorum par, postremo ceteris praelucens apologorum quattuor et uiginti pompa mirabilis. in his quam uariam se praebet et mutabilem: quot uera uanis, quot seria ludicris miscet. quid quod amasios sicut nemo protrahit, seu nulla religione contra nefas obstrictos siue in alternos adfectus desultorio tamquam certamine ruentes? apage istos emunctae naris criticos quibus haec ficta nescioquid maius uelle uideantur. nam eadem nos homunculos ipsa uoluptate, ipsa ueritate deuinciunt. nonne, quae sit arte plus quam Circaea ualens, ipsum Vlixem fascinet? nonne Aristoteles, si *Caput Abscissum* Dionysiis spectasset, metu et misericordia cor concussus foret? immo cum tot pectoris furias, tot incestos et insanos amores lectitamus, quid iam miramur *Cur Plato Fabulantes Exterminauerit*? ne plura: ueris instar quotannis reuertitur, reuersuram quotannis opperimur. nec secus ac maiores obuiam tabellariis effusi proxima Caroli nostri scripta rapiebant, sic nosmet ipsi Sosiorum tabernas animis arrectis obsidemus quo librum quemque nouissimum tempestiuius occupemus, uotique tandem compotes immortalem illam conclamationem Θάλαττα Θάλαττα redintegramus.

Praesento uobis Excellentissimi Ordinis Imperii Britannici Dominam Commendatricem, Collegii Newnhamensis honoris causa Sociam,

JEAN IRIS MURDOCH

[1] Vergil, *Aeneid*, 4. 700–2.

*S*O *Iris on her saffron wings through heaven*
Glides dewy down, trailing a thousand hues
That sparkle in the sun.

At both ends of the rainbow stands philosophy, the slim Sartre, Romantic
Rationalist *(1954) and the solid* Metaphysics as a Guide to Morals
*(1992). Between these glitter a handful of dramas, a volume of poetry, and
a pair of Platonic dialogues, but above all twenty four novels. In their
pages the subtle and serious play of ideas consorts with a cheerful and
sometimes picaresque comedy, and an outwardly realistic world goes hand
in hand with an inner world of illusion and fantasy. Her characters fall in
love across barriers of age and sex usually assumed impassable, or change
partners in a kind of ritualised dance. Academic critics are prone to ascribe
some deeply symbolic meaning to this behaviour, but the common reader is
content to find it fascinating, and even lifelike. She is a binder of spells
more potent than Circe: so that Ulysses himself would take* Flight from
the Enchanter. *What pity and fear would have riven the breast of
Aristotle, if* A Severed Head *had been played in Athens. Indeed, when we
read her imbroglios of passion and madness, need we wonder* Why Plato
banished the Artists? *She has become, like the seasons, an annual miracle.
And as once they lined the streets to snatch from the courier the next
chapters of Dickens, so we await her newest book, then cry, like the troops
of Xenophon after their long march,* The Sea, The Sea.

I present to you

Dame JEAN IRIS MURDOCH,

Honorary Fellow of Newnham College.

Lightning Source UK Ltd.
Milton Keynes UK
28 January 2011

166568UK00001B/20/P